Gustav
KLIMT

Gustav
KLIMT

Edmund Swinglehurst

THUNDER BAY
P·R·E·S·S

First Published in 2001 by
Thunder Bay Press
An imprint of the Advantage Publishers Group
5880 Oberlin Drive, San Diego, CA 92121-4794
www.advantagebooksonline.com

ISBN 1-57145-271-0
Library of Congress Cataloging-in-Publication Data
available upon request.

Printed in Hong Kong

1 2 3 4 5 00 01 02 03 04

ACKNOWLEDGEMENTS
P. 6, Österreichische Nationalbibliotek, Vienna, P. 7, Österreischische Nationalbibliotek, Vienna: P. 8, Österreischische Nationalbibliotek, Vienna: P. 9, Historisches Museum der Stadt, Vienna: P. 10, Österreischische Nationalbibliotek, Vienna: P. 11, Tiroler Landsmuseum Ferdinandeum, Innsbruck: P. 12–13, Historisches Museum der Stadt, Vienna, Austria/Bridgeman Art Library: P. 14–15, Historisches Museum der Stadt, Vienna, Austria/Bridgeman Art Library: P. 16–17, Historisches Museum der Stadt, Vienna, Austria/Bridgeman Art Library: P. 18–21, Kunsthistorisches Museum, Vienna, Austria/Bridgeman Art Library: P. 22, Naródní Galerie, Prague, Czech Republic/Bridgeman Art Library: P. 23, Private Collection/Bridgeman Art Library: P. 25, Kunsthistorisches Museum, Vienna, Austria/Bridgeman Art Library: P. 26, Historisches Museum der Stadt, Vienna, Austria/Bridgeman Art Library: P. 27, Historisches Museum der Stadt, Vienna, Austria/Bridgeman Art Library: P. 28, Private Collection/Bridgeman Art Library: P. 30, Private Collection/Bridgeman Art Library, Credit: The Stapleton Collection: P. 31, Historisches Museum der Stadt, Vienna, Austria/Bridgeman Art Library: P. 32, Private Collection/Bridgeman Art Library: P. 33 left, Private Collection/Bridgeman Art Library, P. 33 right, Private Collection/Bridgeman Art Library: P. 34, Österreichische Galerie, Vienna, Austria/Bridgeman Art Library: P. 35, Private Collection/Bridgeman Art Library: P. 36, Historisches Museum der Stadt, Vienna, Austria/Bridgeman Art Library: P. 37, Private Collection/Bridgeman Art Library: P. 38, Historisches Museum der Stadt, Vienna, Austria/Bridgeman Art Library: P. 41, Österreichische Galerie, Vienna, Austria/Bridgeman Art Library: P. 42 left, Historisches Museum der Stadt, Vienna, Austria: P. 42 right, Österreichische Galerie, Vienna, Austria: P. 43, Private Collection/Bridgeman Art Library: P. 44, Private Collection/Bridgeman Art Library: P. 45, Österreichische Nationalbibliothek, Vienna, Austria/Bridgeman Art Library: P. 47, Historisches Museum der Stadt, Vienna, Austria: P. 48, Private Collection/Bridgeman Art Library: P. 50, Scottish National Gallery of Modern Art, Edinburgh, UK/Bridgeman Art Library: P. 51, Kunstmuseum Solothurn, Switzerland/Bridgeman Art Library, Credit: RMN/Bulloz: P. 52, Österreichische Galerie, Vienna, Austria/Bridgeman Art Library: P. 53, Österreichische Galerie, Vienna, Austria/Bridgeman Art Library: P. 54, Schloss Immendorf, Austria/Bridgeman Art Library: P. 56, Österreichische Galerie, Vienna, Austria/Bridgeman Art Library: P. 58, Galleria Nazionale d'Arte, Rome: P. 60, Private Collection/Bridgeman Art Library: P. 62, 63, Stoclet Palace, Brussels: P. 64, Österreichische Galerie, Vienna, Austria/Bridgeman Art Library: P. 66, Österreichische Galerie, Vienna, Austria/Bridgeman Art Library: P. 67, Palais Stoclet, Brussels, Belgium/Bridgeman Art Library, Credit: Peter Willi: P. 68, Österreichische Galerie, Vienna, Austria/Bridgeman Art Library: P. 70, Österreichische Galerie, Vienna, Austria/Bridgeman Art Library: P. 72, Private Collection/Bridgeman Art Library: P. 74, Museo d'Arte Moderna, Venice, Italy/Bridgeman Art Library: P. 76, Private Collection/Bridgeman Art Library: P. 78, Naródní Galerie, Prague, Czech Republic/Bridgeman Art Library: P. 80, Österreichische Galerie, Vienna, Austria/Bridgeman Art Library: P. 82, Metropolitan Museum of Art, New York: P. 83, The National Gallery, London, UK/Bridgeman Art Library: P. 84, Historisches Museum der Stadt, Vienna, Austria/Bridgeman Art Library: P. 86, National Gallery of Canada, Ottawa: P. 88, Osterreichische Galerie, Vienna, Austria/Bridgeman Art Library: P. 90, Neue Pinakothek, Munich: P. 92, Fischer Fine Art Ltd., London, UK/Bridgeman Art Library: P. 95, Österreichische Galerie, Vienna, Austria: P. 96, Österreichische Galerie, Vienna, Austria: P. 98, Private Collection/Bridgeman Art Library: P. 99, The Metropolitan Museum of Art: P. 100, Österreichisches Galerie, Vienna, Austria/Bridgeman Art Library: P. 102, Österreichisches Galerie, Vienna, Austria: P. 103, Neue Galerie, Linz, Austria/Bridgeman Art Library: P. 104 left, Private Collection/Bridgeman Art Library: P. 104 right, Private Collection/Bridgeman Art Library: P. 105, Private Collection/Bridgeman Art Library: P. 107 above, Private Collection/Bridgeman Art Library: P. 107 below, Private Collection/Bridgeman Art Library: P. 108 top, Private Collection/Bridgeman Art Library: P. 108 below, Private Collection/Bridgeman Art Library: P. 109, Private Collection/Bridgeman Art Library: P. 110, Private Collection/Bridgeman Art Library: P. 111 left, Private Collection/Bridgeman Art Library: P. 111 right, Private Collection/Bridgeman Art Library: P. 112 top, Private Collection/Bridgeman Art Library: P. 112 below, Private Collection/Bridgeman Art Library: P. 113, Private Collection/Bridgeman Art Library: P. 114, Gemäldegalerie Neue Meister, Dresden: P. 115, Österreichische Galerie, Vienna, Austria: P. 116–117, Österreichische Galerie, Vienna, Austria/Bridgeman Art Library: P. 118, Musée d'Orsay, Paris, France/Bridgeman Art Library, Credit: Giraudon/Bridgeman Art Library: P. 120–121, Busch-Reisinger Museum, Harvard University Art Museums, USA/Bridgeman Art Library, Gift of Otto Kallir: P. 122–123, Österreichisches Galerie, Vienna, Austria: P. 124, Österreichisches Galerie, Vienna, Austria: P. 126, Private Collection/Bridgeman Art Library: P. 128, Österreichisches Galerie, Vienna, Austria: P. 130–131, Österreichisches Galerie, Vienna, Austria: P. 132, Österreichisches Galerie, Vienna, Austria: P. 133, Österreichisches Galerie, Vienna, Austria: P. 134, Heydt Museum, Wuppertal, Germany/Bridgeman Art Library: P. 135, Österreichisches Galerie, Vienna, Austria/Bridgeman Art Gallery: P. 136–137, Österreichische Galerie, Vienna, Austria/Bridgeman Art Library: P. 138, Fitzwilliam Museum, University of Cambridge, UK/Bridgeman Art Library: P. 140–141, Private Collection/Bridgeman Art Library: P. 142, Private Collection/Bridgeman Art Library CREDIT: Marlborough Graphics, London, UK: P. 143, Museum of Fine Arts, Boston, Mass., USA/Bridgeman Art Library.

Contents

CHAPTER ONE

THE VIENNESE SCENE

During the lifetime of Gustav Klimt, the Austrian Jugendstil (Art Nouveau) painter, the Austro-Hungarian Empire began its transition from a sprawling, outmoded political dinosaur, stretched across eastern Europe to the Adriatic, into a compact modern state. The political, economic and cultural life of the nation all saw many changes and Klimt himself was one of the instigators of new forms and styles in art.

Gustav Klimt was born in 1862 in the Vienna suburb of Baumgarten. Just four years later, the mighty Austrian army suffered a humiliating defeat at the hands of the Prussians at the Battle of Sadowa (Königgrätz) in the Seven Weeks War. The shock of defeat, unknown in Austria since the defeat by Napoleon at Austerlitz in 1805, caused a national trauma felt nowhere more severely than at the court of the Emperor Franz Joseph I.

BELOW

Gustav Klimt in the garden of his studio

Österreichische Nationalbibliothek, Vienna.

Klimt's first studio was in a simple one-storey house in one of the workers' districts of Vienna. Here he was able to work in seclusion, wearing a monkish robe for comfort, while also attending classes at the art school.

OPPOSITE

Gustav Klimt

Österreichische Nationalbibliothek, Vienna.

As a well known painter of murals in public buildings, Klimt assumed an appearance appropriate to his position. Even his beard and moustache were trimmed to a fashionable shape. However, he later rejected the conventions of Viennese society.

Until 1866, the Austrian Empire had remained
cocooned in its past, ignoring the revolutionary changes
occurring in the rest of Europe. In Austria, the Court was
the social arbiter, the Army kept order and provided a career
for the sons of the bourgeoisie, and the Church set the
moral tone to which the nation was expected to adhere. Art
came largely under the control of the Academy of Fine Arts
which encouraged paintings of predominantly classical
subjects.

During Klimt's youth, changes were already beginning
to appear. A parliament with limited powers was set up; the
franchise was widened; Jews and Czechs, formerly excluded
from political and commercial life, were emancipated; and
marriage into a class other than one's own was now
condoned. And as if to symbolize these changes, a broad
new boulevard, the Ringstrasse, was built around the old
centre of Vienna, the Empire's capital city.

The new mood of the Viennese people manifested itself
in a passion for entertainment which spread throughout

OPPOSITE

Joseph Maria-Olbrich (left) with Kolomon Moser, Gustave Klimt (both on reclining chairs) and an unidentified person, photographed in Klimt's garden.

Österreichische Nationalbibliothek, Vienna.

The modernist artists of Vienna met frequently and planned how to break the hold of the art establishment on public taste by control of places where artists could exhibit. In this photograph, Klimt is shown with Kolomon Moser, an architect and interior decorator, Joseph-Maria Olbrich, a graphic designer, and an unidentified person, all of whom joined the Secession of 1898 and set up their own exhibition gallery.

LEFT

Male Nude in Walking Posture, from the Right
(1877–1879)
Pencil, heightened with white. 17 x 10²/₃in (43 x 27cm). Historisches Museum der Stadt, Vienna.

This male nude in a typically academic pose was produced by Klimt as a study for the kind of figures he used in his conventional mural paintings for theatres and public buildings.

society and had its own signature tune – the waltz – which the Viennese took to their hearts, its three-beats-to-the-bar rhythm sounding not only in the Imperial palace but also in cafés, restaurants, beer gardens and parks, its strains filling the air in spring when there were Fasching balls for every level of society, from the Imperial army to cabdrivers' and laundrywomen's cooperatives.

This explosion of *joie de vivre* provided an abundance of talent: Johann Strauss was providing hundreds of waltzes and several operettas while Arthur Schnitzler, who was the Noel Coward of his day, poured out risqué comedies reflecting society as it now was, with all its social peccadilloes. Emilie Flöge was designing dresses which hung loosely from the shoulders and no longer squeezed the life out of women previously imprisoned in stays and corsets, while architects and designers such as Josef Hoffmann and Koloman Moser

9

were planning a new architecture which would no longer be rooted in the past. Moreover, Gustav Mahler, after his studies at the Vienna Conservatory, was composing symphonies which were beginning to express the more profound changes now taking place in the world.

Such were the people who made up Klimt's world, many of them becoming his lifelong friends, while another, not known to him personally but who exerted a powerful influence on his thought and art, was Sigmund Freud, born in Austria six years before Klimt himself. Freud's career began in neurology, but he later developed an interest in psychopathology, devoting his life to the investigation of the subconscious mind which led to his theory that the sexual

drive was the prime motivater of almost all human activity.

The realm of the arts was one of the last cultural activities to manifest change: although there were new developments in Dresden, Munich and Berlin, the Viennese art establishment was restrictive of young artists, its head firmly set against forms of art of which it disapproved. This was therefore the challenge facing Klimt and his colleagues at the start of their careers, but although his work initially complied with the requirements of his patrons, Klimt soon began to develop his own ideas when, with his friends Carl Moll and Josef Englehart, he planned an association of artists who would break away from the establishment and create their own artistic environment.

ABOVE

The Austrian Museum of Art and Industry

Österreichische Nationalbibliothek, Vienna.

Klimt began his career as a student at the School of Applied Art attached to the Austrian Museum of Art and Industry.

ABOVE

Portrait of Joseph Pembauer (1890)

Oil on canvas. 27 x 21²/₃in (69 x 55cm). Tiroler Landsmuseum Ferdinandeum, Innsbruck.

The stylized lyre in the background of the portrait indicates that Joseph Pembauer was a musician, which indeed he was. He was a pianist and counted Klimt and the great composer Gustav Mahler among his friends. The frame surrounding the picture is also highly decorated and includes a man standing on a classical column, playing another lyre.

CHAPTER TWO

THE EARLY YEARS

Gustav Klimt came from a family of craftsmen – simple people who worked hard and long for a living. His father was a goldsmith, his brother, Ernst, became a painter and his brother Georg a sculptor and engraver. Gustav's mother kept house though she was a semi-invalid beset by psychological problems, a fact which haunted Klimt all his life and was the probable cause of his own hypochondria. Apart from this, the family was happy enough, and Klimt's younger sister Hermine recalled many years later that her brother had been fond of keeping rabbits, had a good appetite, and did well at school.

The family, which was not well off, found its financial situation deteriorating after the Vienna stockmarket crashed in 1873, which obliged the boys to seek work while they were still at the School of Applied Art, an establishment where, unlike the Academy of Fine Arts, art was taught as a practical subject, as a craft which applied as much to

Fable (1883)
Oil on canvas. 33¼ x 46in (84.5 x 117cm). Historisches Museum der Stadt, Vienna.

The fable referred to in the title is not an instructional story in the manner of Aesop or La Fontaine, but an allegorical reference to the relationship between humanity and the natural world. At this point in history, the intelligentsia of western Europe regarded animals and even primitive peoples as inhabiting a kind of Eden set on earth, intended solely for their enjoyment and exploitation. People did not dwell too deeply on whatever feelings animals might possess, but regarded them as objects to be hunted, or at best kept as domestic pets. At the same time, and according to the mores of the times, the use of fables and myths in paintings distanced the present from the past and provided an excellent opportunity of displaying the nude female body in the accepted classical manner.

·IDYLLE·

Idyll (1884)
Oil on canvas. 19½ x 29in (49.5 x 73.5cm). Historisches Museum der Stadt, Vienna.

This conventional picture was painted during the time that Klimt was illustrating the book *Allegorien und Embleme*. Its graphic composition of two lateral figures and a central medallion was used in Renaissance art and Klimt's inspiration for the figures obviously comes from Michelangelo, though with none of that great artist's power. This was the kind of art acceptable to those who commissioned the work and which prompted Klimt to rebel against the Establishment's views.

everyday and domestic objects as to objets d'art, paintings and sculptures. This practical grounding was to be the foundation for much of Klimt's work and inspired his support of movements uniting art with everyday life.

Though times were hard, Klimt was able to stay on at the school with the help of an official grant, another recipient of such a bursary being Franz Matsch, who was to become a close friend and collaborator for many years. Both youths were exceptionally talented and received the support and encouragement of their teachers, who helped them to find professional work as assistants and draughtsmen: on one occasion, Klimt was asked to prepare diagrams for a well-known ear specialist. They also assisted Professor Adam Rieser with his designs for windows in Vienna's Votivkirche.

Their greatest success, however, came when their teachers recommended them to Hans Makart, a celebrated Viennese entrepreneur and designer who was a showman *par excellence* and dressed with a panache and style reflecting his flamboyant lifestyle. He liked to throw extravagant fancy dress parties to which Viennese society were invited, with those likely to commission work very much in evidence, and he was a frequent visitor at the Emperor's court.

Through his imperial connections, Makart was able to acquire the most sought-after commission of 1879, that of designing the procession for the Silver Wedding celebrations of the Emperor Franz Joseph and the Empress Elisabeth. This was intended to include all of the inhabitants of Vienna, from the highest to the lowest, and was to be spread out along the whole of the Ringstrasse.

The Auditorium (1888) Gouache on paper. 32¼ x 36¼in (82 x 92cm). Historisches Museum der Stadt, Vienna.

Klimt and his friend Franz Matsch were both commissioned to decorate the old Burgtheater in Vienna, but Klimt's assignment was more difficult for he was also asked to paint it and to include the socialites of Vienna. He managed to do so, filling the balcony spaces with his own family and friends, and the Emperor Franz Joseph was so impressed by the result that he awarded him 400 guilders. The success of the painting did much to enhance Klimt's reputation.

The procession was to be the main event of the festivities and would include decorated floats, troupes of dancers, bands, tableaux, performers of all kinds as well as set pieces strung along the route. These would be designed by Makart and his team of designers and decorators, among them Gustav Klimt and Franz Matsch. For students to be so involved was deemed a great honour and served to bring the young men to the public's attention. Klimt was also struck with Shakespeare's insight into human nature when he wrote, 'All the world's a stage ....'

Encouraged by the high opinion of their teachers and others for whom they had carried out minor projects, the Klimt brothers and Matsch formed themselves into a team called the Künstlercompagnie through which, though still involved in their studies, they were able to establish a commercial identity by which they could undertake more work. Consequently, and shortly after the Emperor's anniversary, they were invited to design and execute ceiling paintings at the Kurhaus in Carlsbad (Karlovy Vary). The commission came through the architects Feliner and Helmer, who had designed the Carlsbad State Theatre and were seeking artists to decorate the ceiling, which meant working within the parameters of historicist themes, still prevalent at the time, and in a traditional Beaux Arts manner. This was well within the capabilities of Klimt and Matsch and the ceiling was completed to everyone's satisfaction.

Carlsbad was an important spa town patronized by the wealthy and well-connected, not only for the curative powers of its waters but also for its importance as a social

rendezvous. The project was crucial in that the young artists of the Künstlercompagnie were able to gain recognition in their own right and they hoped that further commissions to decorate private houses would come their way. However, the main benefit of such a commission was the opportunity to meet the architects who had built the Kurhaus and who would be responsible for other important buildings.

But Klimt knew that decorating provincial theatres was hardly going to establish his reputation in Vienna and, encouraged by his success so far, he and Matsch took a studio at Sandwirthgasse in the capital in 1883. Although this now became the headquarters of the two friends' business, it did not provide enough income to pay the rent, so Klimt and Matsch took on other work, including the decoration of the National Theatre at Bucharest, and a

ABOVE and OPPOSITE
The interior of the
Kunsthistorisches
Museum, Vienna
(1890–91)

In order to represent the theme of 14th- and 15th-century Florence, Klimt incorporated the figures of David and Venus into his design. Many of the more important spaces in the museum had been

decorated by the most famous and fashionable Viennese designer, Makart, and Klimt was faced with the problem of filling the awkward spandrels in the best way that he could. It was an honour to be chosen to provide work which would be seen alongside that of Makart and Klimt seized the opportunity with enthusiasm.

The interior of the Kunsthistorisches Museum, Vienna (1890–91)

The themes of the spandrels on the doorways in the museum were drawn from classical history and, as with most commissioned work, Klimt was expected to follow orders. The choice of personages in the painting was left to him so he chose Minerva, goddess of wisdom, whose original Greek name was Pallas Athene. Her style of dress has ancient origins and she holds a statue of Nike (Victory) and a spear as symbols of power. In the Egyptian spandrel he also chose a goddess, probably Isis, wife of the god Osiris, holding an *ankh*, the symbol of life. Unusually, however, Klimt depicts her as a full frontal nude.

RIGHT
Portrait of a Young Woman (c.1896)
Pencil. Národní Gallery, Prague.

This unknown woman may have been one of Klimt's girlfriends, though he met many women though his family and clientele and some of them were his models. However, his attitude to women was very much conditioned by the social mores of his time but he was known for his kindness and gentility towards all women, whatever their relationship to him.

OPPOSITE
Study of the Head of a Blind Man (c. 1898)
Oil on canvas. 26 x 21in (67 x 53cm). Private collection.

Klimt made two studies of this man who most likely was paid to pose for him as a model This one was exhibited at the first Secessionist exhibition of 1898. However, its present location is unknown, though it is possibly now in private hands. It is hoped that it was not lost during the war, like much of Klimt's other work.

theatre in Fiume. There were also private commissions, including the decoration of private villas and the illustration of an important volume on allegories and symbols for the publisher Martin Gerlach. The volume featured the work of all artists who had used these two forms of expression and Klimt's contribution continued for several years from 1881.

In preparation for his work on the Carlsbad theatre, Klimt had managed to accumulate a great deal of information as well as various ideas which would be useful in realizing the classical and historical themes considered appropriate by official bodies for the ornamentation of public buildings. This made the Klimt/Matsch partnership a suitable choice for the decoration of the new Burgtheater (p. 16–17) in the Ringstrasse. Backed by their teacher, Eitelberger, the young men managed to win one of the most desirable commissions in Vienna, which would establish

them as the foremost decorators of public buildings in the city.

Klimt and Matsch divided between them the panels that had to be painted, Klimt settling for scenes of The Altar of Dionysus, The Chariot of Thespis, Shakespeare's Globe Theatre, The Greek Theatre of Taormina and The Altar of Apollo. Matsch completed the ceiling paintings with representations of Greek and medieval theatres, while another panel, of the poet Hanswurst reciting his poetry in public, was given to Klimt's brother Ernst, who unfortunately died before it was completed, and it was left for Gustav Klimt to finish it. All the paintings were of a considerable size and painted in the Beaux Arts style, which was the conventional choice for public buildings of the time.

The work's success was assured by the public acclaim it received. When the Emperor Franz Josef thought fit to bestow gold medals on both painters in recognition of their service to Austrian art, there was no doubt that Klimt and Matsch could count themselves among the élite of Vienna's artistic world. But, secretly, Klimt was bitterly disappointed. His intention was to break new ground, but he had ended up still very much in the academic mould of the cultural establishment. At the same time, however, he realized that it would be no easy task to find patrons willing to support progressive and original ideas.

Dissatisfied and restless, Klimt spent the next two years travelling and exploring in his mind avenues which might release him from the impasse of traditional art forms. He visited Cracow, Munich, Trieste (then part of the Austrian Empire) and Venice, where he considered what to do next. He did not visit Paris, where the Impressionists were introducing visionary new concepts to the painter's art. If he had, he may very well have found the scene all too radical to comprehend, coming as he did from a world still very much trapped in the past.

Love (1895)
Oil on canvas. 23⁵/₈ x 17³/₈in (60 x 44cm). Kunsthistorisches Museum, Vienna.

In his youth, Klimt had the usual conventional ideas concerning the nature of romantic love then prevalent in Viennese society. This reflected the mood of the times when women either stood aloof and unattainable as middle-class goddesses, or had been put on earth simply to be exploited by men. In this painting, Klimt reflects the romantic delusions of those who commissioned his work.

RIGHT

**Detail of a Boy in
Medieval Costume**

(Franz Matsch, 1906)

Oil on canvas.

Historisches Museum der
Stadt. Vienna

This young man wearing
an historical costume, the
work of Franz Matsch, is
in much the same style
as figures Klimt included
in his decorations of
public buildings, where
requirements reflected
the traditional and
conventional. The richly
patterned background
points the direction that
Klimt was to take once he
had broken loose from
the Establishment and
had found patrons who
were willing to support
his more progressive
work.

OPPOSITE

Portrait of a Lady

(c. 1894)

Oil on wood. 12 x 9in
(30 x 23cm). Historisches
Museum der Stadt,
Vienna.

This unknown woman
may be a Frau Heymann,
according to art historian
F. Gluck. Klimt, like most
artists at the beginning of
their careers, undoubtedly
asked his friends to pose
for him. This portrait,
however, is very
conventional and is
painted using a tonal
technique. Though
photography had by this
time come into use, an oil
painting still had a certain
cachet among the social
élite.

On his return to Vienna, Klimt was commissioned to
paint murals on the spandrels of the doorways of the
Kunsthistorisches Museum (p. 18–21) but found, once
again, that the specifications were such that they inhibited
freedom of action, though he managed to introduce a novel
pose for the female figures representing the art of Greece
and Egypt. In the Egyptian spandrel, in particular, he paints
a naked female figure in a frontal pose in the Egyptian style,
holding an *ankh* in her right hand, while behind her is the
god, Horus, in symbolic form. Klimt thus introduced two
elements – stylization and symbolism – which would appear
more forcibly and more frequently in his future work.

With his reputation now firmly established, Klimt was
able to join the Künstlerhausgenossenschaft (Cooperative
Society of Artists), the most influential association of artists
in Vienna and a springboard from which a campaign to
change attitudes in art might perhaps be launched. The time
had come not only to expand his business but also to take a
leading part in bringing about a revolution in Viennese art.

Klimt's energy and decision were tempered for a time by

Portrait of a Young Woman (1896)
Pencil drawing.
Private Collection

The attractive young woman in this unfinished sketch may well be Emilie Flöge, who was the wife of Klimt's brother, Ernst. After her husband's death she became one of Klimt's closest companions and a lifelong friend. The flowing line of the drawing was to be a characteristic of Klimt's style which later on came to be identified as Art Nouveau.

two family tragedies – the deaths of his father and, shortly after, his brother Ernst. As Klimt's family had always been close-knit, he felt their deaths deeply, but found comfort in a closer relationship with Ernst's wife, Emilie Flöge, who came to resemble a blood sister.

Once the initial shock and sadness had dissipated, Klimt's energy returned, allowing him to form the plan of setting up a group within the Künstlerhaus which would actively promote the modernization of art. This was not a new idea: in both Dresden and Munich young artists, calling themselves Secessionists, had also grouped together with the intention of breaking away from the existing arts establishments; but in Vienna, where even Impressionism had not yet penetrated, it was a revolutionary concept.

Under the leadership of Klimt, Carl Moll and Josef Englehart, an association was formed in Vienna in 1897 with the name Vereiningung Bildender Künstler Österreiches (Association of Austrian Visual Artists). The association came generally to be known as the 'Secession', the name being adapted from its slogan, *Secesio Plebia in Montem Sacrum*, inspired by the Roman custom of the populace withdrawing to the Mons Sacer when they intended to protest against official attitudes and actions.

The Secession published a magazine called *Ver Sacrum* (The Sacred Spring) in which it announced its manifesto. This declared the Secessionists' belief that all art was one, that there should be no distinction between high art and craft; art was for everyone and they believed that it should not be constricted by rules and regulations. The declaration concluded with two slightly ingenuous exhortations, the first to be unafraid of ridicule and the second to learn to be hated.

These sensitive though self-conscious first steps into a new world of art were cautious because the Secession members were loath to create enemies in the existing art world of Vienna. For this reason, the Secession passed almost

unnoticed in other centres of art: Munich and Dresden had already had their Secessionist exhibitions and in Paris Impressionism was already being overtaken by post-Impressionism and the art of Cézanne and Van Gogh. For the same reason, the first Vienna Secession exhibition in 1898, to which foreign artists, who had hitherto been ignored in official Viennese exhibitions, had been invited, received little support from abroad. There were works by Frank Brangwyn and Walter Crane from England, Auguste Rodin and Puvis de Chavannes from France, and the Americans working in England, John Singer Sargent and James McNeill Whistler, the latter, rather grudgingly, sending a pair of lithographs.

The success of the Secession lay at home. The response of the Viennese people was clear evidence that everyone had been waiting for a change in the outward forms of established art. The exhibition, held in the headquarters of Vienna's Horticultural Association because the only available gallery in Vienna was run by the Künstlerhaus, succeeded commercially. It had 57,000 visitors and sold 218 items out of the 534 exhibited, only one item arousing a protest, which was the exhibition poster which Klimt had designed. He had taken the Minotaur legend as his theme and had shown Theseus completely naked in the act of slaying the monster (p. 36). To placate the authorities, Klimt added the trunk of a tree to hide the offending private parts, and all was well.

The aftermath of the exhibition was no less satisfying. It created a new buying public for the Secessionist painters and ensured there would be backers for a Secessionist museum for future exhibitions. Klimt, who had become the president of the Secession, felt personally triumphant: a door was at last opening onto his future and with James Whistler's recommendation for his membership of the Society of Sculptors, Painters and Engravers in London, he considered himself on the threshold of international recognition.

CHAPTER THREE

A TIME OF TRANSITION

Although the founding of the Secession was an important landmark in the artistic life of Vienna and was regarded as a desirable event, even by the Emperor Franz Joseph, it was not as important to Klimt as the development of his own art. He had been schooled by Makart and his style of traditional painting, variously described by critics as 'Rubensesque, traditional, pompier and laden with overt saccharine teutonic sexuality', left him intending to free himself from these acquired habits.

In the Carlsbad paintings, his attempt at breaking away had resulted in an Alma-Tadema-style modernization of Roman scenes, and in the Burgtheater paintings he had attempted a stylized, two-dimensional technique inspired by ancient frescoes. Neither of these sorties had satisfied him. By now, he was well aware of the developments in France and realized that a completely new way of seeing was necessary.

It was at this stage in his inner conflict that Klimt and his

LEFT

Poster for an exhibition of Secessionist art
(Franz von Stuck, 1893) Lithograph. Private Collection.

This poster is by Klimt's fellow Secessionist, Franz von Stuck, and uses the Pallas Athene symbol which the association of artists had adopted. Stuck first used the motif in a poster for the Munich artists' secession which preceded that of Vienna. It was adopted by the Viennese painters and used in subsequent exhibitions up to the Kandinsky exhibition of 1901. Though the new movement in art was breaking with old techniques and styles, the reverence for classical symbols remained.

OPPOSITE

Tragedy (1897)
Black chalk and pen with gold. 16$^{1}/_{2}$ x 12$^{1}/_{5}$in (42 x 31cm). Historisches Museum der Stadt, Vienna.

The illustrations Klimt produced for *Allegorien und Embleme* were commissioned by the publisher Martin Gerlach. The intention of the work, in three parts, was to provide a complete guide to all the themes real or idealized which had been used throughout the history of art. Gerlach was prepared to allow his artists an artistic freedom not possible in works for public authorities and Klimt produced a series of designs which were to be the forerunners of his later work.

OPPOSITE

Pallas Athene

(Franz von Stuck, 1898)
Oil on panel. 30^{1}/$_{3}$ ×
27^{1}/$_{3}$in (77 × 69.5cm).
Private Collection.

Though the Secessionists
were now actively
rejecting traditional

classical art, they were
still inclined to use the old
symbols. Consequently,
'grey-eyed' Athena, the
Greek goddess of
wisdom, was adopted as
an appropriate icon and
was used throughout all
the Secessionist
movements.

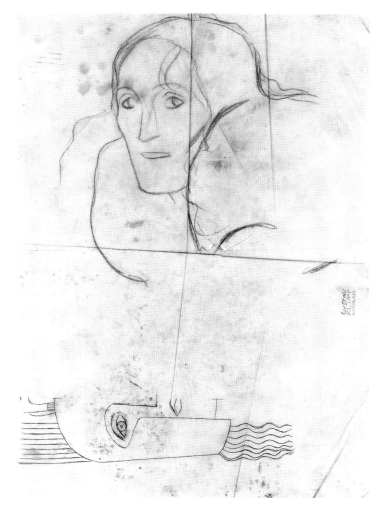

LEFT

An Old Woman (Detail.
1909)
Oil on canvas. 37^{1}/$_{2}$ ×
18^{1}/$_{2}$in (95.3 × 47cm).
Private collection.

This painting coincided
with the period when
Klimt was painting the
lucid two-dimensional
designs for the Stoclet
palace and seems to
indicate that he was
seeking for a way to
return to a style with
greater emotional content
and satisfaction.

ABOVE

Studies for *Ver Sacrum*

(Pallas Athene and a tragic
head,1897–98)
Pencil and blue crayon on
paper. 14^{1}/$_{2}$ × 22in (37 ×
56cm). Private collection.

The Viennese
Secessionists announced
their ideas through a
magazine called *Ver
Sacrum*, The Sacred
Spring, supposedly a place
to which the ancient
Romans retired to express
their dissatisfactions with
the *status quo*.

Sonja Knips (1898)
Oil on canvas. 57 x 57in
(145 x 145cm)
Österreichische Galerie,
Vienna.

This is a portrait of a woman who, with her husband Antonio, became a leading light in the Vienna Werkstätte, founded in 1903 by Josef Hoffmann and Kolomon Moser, which advanced the views of the Secessionists. It is painted on a square canvas which was to become one of Klimt's trademarks. The portrait is in the Impressionist style with which Klimt was experimenting as he detached himself from the traditional academicism of his youth.

Seated Woman (Study for a portrait of Sonja Knips, 1898)
Blue crayon on paper. 18 x 12¹/₂in (45.7 x 31.8cm). Private collection.

This study was a preliminary sketch for the portrait of Sonja Knips opposite. However, the drawing is rather tentative, with lines drawn in twice as if Klimt were searching for an outline that satisfied him. After years of precise academic draughtsmanship he needed to loosen up his drawing in order to project a feeling of atmosphere and ambience.

partner Matsch drifted apart. Matsch was happy with what he was doing, but Klimt was infected by the restless and exploratory spirit which was abroad, heralding a new artistic age. His paintings were now beginning to assume an Impressionist and distinctly atmospheric timbre.

In his 1898 portrait of Sonja Knips, for example, he has dispensed with the hard outlines of his academic paintings and allowed the young woman's pink dress to fade gently into the background, which he has left empty of the props of traditional convention. In another painting of the same period, which would hang in the music room of the Dumba Palace, he paints Schubert in an Impressionist style by candlelight at the piano, surrounded by admiring young women (p. 46). Given similar treatment is a portrait of

OPPOSITE
Cover of *Ver Sacrum*
(1888/9)
Lithograph. Historisches
Museum der Stadt,
Vienna.

The Secessionists, who
were trying to establish a
more modern style of art
in Vienna, published a
magazine to promote
their ideas. They chose
the name *Ver Sacrum* (The
Sacred Spring) and
provided illustrations for it.
This first cover by Klimt
with the theme of
Theseus and the Minotaur
shocked the Viennese
because Theseus' private
parts were exposed for all
to see. A tree trunk was
later added for so-called
modesty's sake.

Serena Lederer (p. 82), the wife of an admirer of Klimt's
paintings who was to become a collector of his work.

The new style that Klimt was adopting to enable him to
escape from his Makart conditioning was softer, less
dogmatic than the accepted art of the past and reflected the
uncertainties that lay beneath the optimistic façade of
contemporary Vienna. The new mood was concealed by the
gaiety of the waltz and the hectic whirl of theatres and cafés,
but it was there beneath the surface, between the lines of the
writings of Sigmund Freud and in the music of Gustav
Mahler.

In Klimt's work, the life beneath the surface emerged as
a preoccupation with symbolism, a subject that Sigmund
Freud had explored in 1901 in his book *The Interpretation of
Dreams*. Klimt had long been interested in legendary and
mythological interpretations of reality since illustrating the
book *Allegorien und Embleme*. He had made use of

ABOVE
The Blood of Fish (1898)
Engraving.
Private Collection.

This elegant drawing first
appeared in *Ver Sacrum*
and demonstrates the
flowing lines associated
with Art Nouveau, an art
style which swept
Europe and America and
which seems to have
spawned a spontaneous
eruption of taste in many
countries and penetrated
art, architecture, fashion,
furnishings, and every
other aspect of social
life. Much of
Secessionist art was
imbued with the spirit of
Art Nouveau and the
drawing reveals one of
Klimt's early obsessions
in which he uses the
female body as a means
of expressing an idea.

Minerva or **Pallas Athene** (1898) Oil on canvas. 29$\frac{1}{2}$ x 29$\frac{1}{2}$in (75 x 75cm). Historisches Museum der Stadt, Vienna.

Pallas Athene, the Greek goddess of wisdom was re-named Minerva by the Romans when they adopted the Greek pantheon, romanizing most of the Olympians in the manner of all powerful imperial nations. For Klimt, Pallas Athene was a convenient symbol to which he gave a new meaning by the innovative image he created. Here, the goddess has a portentous appearance, her helmet producing the semblance of a death's head. Between her breasts is the face of the Medusa with her tongue protruding, and the small nude on the left suggests vulnerable humanity.

symbolism in his Burgtheater murals and in his painting of
Pallas Athene. In this, the goddess wears an imposing
helmet which covers her face, leaving her deep-set eyes in
shadow, and producing the effect of a death's head. On her
golden coin breastplate there is a face of Medusa with the
tongue protruding and in the orb in Athena's right hand is
a nude figure, possibly symbolizing the frailty of humanity.

Klimt's interest in symbolism is evident in his paintings
Acqua Mossa of 1898, and *Bische d'Acqua* and *Nuda Veritas*
(p. 42), both 1899. But themes were only a part of his
artistic concern: he was very much preoccupied with style
and technique. He had become aware of the art emanating
from Paris and the influence on the work of the
Impressionists of Japanese art, the flat, two-dimensional
designs and the new spatial relations being inconceivable
where traditional techniques, where perspective and
chiaroscuro played a dominant role, still prevailed.

As he meditated on these new concepts, Klimt began to
plan the murals that had been commissioned for the Great

Judith I (1901)
Oil on canvas with gold.
33 x 16½in (84 x 42cm).
Österreichische Galerie,
Vienna.

Judith, who assassinated
Nebuchadnezzar's
general, Holofernes,
whose army was
threatening the town of
Bethulia, where Judith's
people had their home, is
one of the epic stories of
the Bible and has served
many artists as a theme
for paintings. Klimt chose
not to depict the murder
but shows Judith as the
epitome of powerful
womanhood, beautiful
and luxuriously dressed in
gold; however, she is
holding the severed head
of Holofernes in her right
hand.

(See also *Judith II* on
pages 74 and 75, which is
also known as *Salome*,
the themes of both being
similar.)

LEFT

Finished drawing for
Nuda Veritas (1898)
Black chalk, pencil, pen
and brush, using Indian
ink.16 x 4in (41 x 10cm).
Historisches Museum der
Stadt, Vienna.

This was another drawing
produced for *Ver Sacrum*
in which the quotation by
Schefer over the head of
the naked woman holding
a mirror translates as:
'Truth is Fire, Truth means
Illumination and Burning'.
The woman is a symbol
of the Secessionist
intention of clearing away
the stagnant ideas of the
past and moving forward
to a new interpretation of
art and life.

RIGHT

Nuda Veritas (1899)
Oil on canvas. 99^{1}/$_{4}$ x 22in
(252 x 56cm).
Österreichische
Nationalbibliothek,
Vienna.

This was painted a year
after the drawing on the
left and is a version in oils
which is not stylized but
painted with an
Impressionist technique.

Musik (1901)
Woodcut.
Private collection.

Music was a theme that Klimt adopted for an illustration in *Allegorien und Embleme*. He also produced other paintings of the same subject of a woman with a lyre, a conventional cultural symbol. This woodcut is derived from the various other works on the subject: the woman is wearing a classical Greek chiton which later inspired a more casual style of dress among Viennese fashion houses, including that of Emilie Flöge. Klimt himself often wore a loose robe while working in his studio.

Poster for Secessionist Exhibition (Alfred Roller, 1902)
Private collection.

By the time of the Secessionist's 14th exhibition, the art styles of the various members had changed. The influence of other European art movements which Secessionist

pressure had made accessible in Vienna by exhibitions of the art of other countries, had had its effect. This poster, produced for the exhibition based on the Klinger Beethoven statue, shows the influence of developments in design pioneered by William Morris.

Monograms of nine Jugendstil artists

(1900s). Österreichische Nationalbibliothek, Vienna.

The artists who formed themselves into an association with the purpose of escaping from the stagnant official art of the past believed that their work should penetrate every aspect of social activity, and this included the crafts which had hitherto been

LEOPOLD BAUER   ADOLF BÖHM   JOSEF HOFFMANN

GUSTAV KLIMT   FRIEDRICH KÖNIG   RICHARD LUKSCH

KOLOMAN MOSER   ALFRED ROLLER   ERNST STÖHR

74

regarded simply as trades. Their enthusiasm carried them into the realms of printing and typography and in order to identify themselves in a new way, each artist designed his own logo. In this print are included the monograms of Leopold Bauer, Adolf Böhm, Josef Hoffmann, Gustav Klimt., Friedrich König, Richard Luksch, Koloman Moser, Alfred Roller and Ernst Stöhr.

Hall of the University. The project had been suggested to the Künstlercompagnie in 1894 by the Ministry of Education and it now needed to be expedited with sketches of the planned murals submitted for the approval of the University. The fee for the sketches was 6000 florins which would be paid to the Künstlercompagnie, Klimt's share of the work being to produce suitable ceiling murals on the subjects of *Medicine*, *Philosophy* and *Jurisprudence*. In 1898 Klimt presented his cartoons for approval by the Beaux Arts committee who suggested amendments. But when he made changes and re-presented his work, he came up against more criticism of his design for *Jurisprudence*.

This was the beginning of a series of attacks on his work which included criticism by a section of the University professors who demanded to know why public money was being spent on such unsuitable work. Some of the critics, quoting a new German law on immorality in art, found the nude women in the paintings offensive. After several years'

work, during which the panel on *Philosophy* had been shown at the seventh exhibition of the Secession and won a Grand Prix at the Paris World Fair, Klimt's patience at last ran out and he offered to buy back his work, which led to further disputes regarding the ownership of the paintings when they eventually came into the possession of Klimt's friend, August Lederer, who installed them in his country mansion where they were destroyed in a fire during the German retreat in 1945.

The cartoons and sketches of the work remain and it is difficult to see why they aroused such a furore. Klimt had attempted to express the concept of the three faculties in a symbolic manner but the technique was not unduly unconventional when perceived as a work in the style of an 18-century mural painter. The hard outlines of the traditional Beaux Arts style were dissolved in a background of airy skies and clouds; naked women represented human qualities through mythological divinities as they had always

done, but Klimt gave them a new meaning. In the *Medicine* panel, the bland caring angel of compassion becomes Hygieia, goddess of medicine (p. 54 and 55), standing before a column of the sick and dying behind which hovers the figure of Death. The whole panel has a cloudy impressionistic quality expressing the mystery of life and death before which the science of medicine is ultimately powerless.

The efforts of *Philosophy* to unravel the puzzle of existence received similarly uncompromising treatment from Klimt. The action of the painting takes place in a space filled with nebulae and stars, from which a shadowy woman's head stares out at a column of naked human figures. Klimt himself did not try to explain the meaning of his painting: like Picasso some years later, he claimed that the meaning lay in the painting itself and did not need his verbal explanation.

The critic and art historian, Ludwig Hevesi, made some attempt to enlighten bewildered art lovers by telling them that what they were looking at in Klimt's *Philosophy* was 'a piece

Schubert at the Piano
(1899)
Oil on canvas. 59 x 78³/₄in (150 x 200cm). Originally situated above the door of the music room of the Nikolaus Dumba Palace. Destroyed by a fire at the Immendorf Palace in 1945.

This realistic portait of Franz Schubert was taken from a watercolour by Leopold Kupelwieser who had painted the great composer when he was alive. Klimt's intention was to distance himself from historicism to create a mood and ambience in which Schubert would have entertained the assembled gathering, the candlelight reflected on their faces.

of the universe in mysterious fermentation', and spoke of cosmic dust, whirling atoms, and elemental forces. 'Shining children,' he wrote, 'bodies in the first bloom of youth, which embrace, experience desire and misery, work, conflict, struggle, the suffering of human life and finally its passing. The lonely old man with his head in his hands, sinks down to the depths like an empty shell.'

Such an interpretation, close as it may have been to Klimt's intentions, was not likely to inspire the acceptance of his paintings in a society devoted to the gaiety and comfortable living of this decadent era, and it is possible that it only added to the barrage of attacks on the painter.

Klimt's painting for *Jurisprudence* must have been an even more upsetting affront to public taste. In it, the figure of an old man, a sinner or a criminal, is enveloped in an octopus-like creature and surrounded by three distorted harpy-like female figures; in a secondary background scene are the clothed figures of *Law*, *Justice* and *Truth*. For this painting, Klimt has adopted a hard-edged style and makes no effort to place the figures in a three-dimensional space. All the elements of the picture are incised against a flat black background and treated decoratively. This was the beginning of a style that Klimt was to develop and perfect for the rest of his life.

Finished drawing for

Envy (1898) Black chalk, pencil, pen and brush, using Indian ink. 16 x 4in (41 x 10cm). Historisches Museum der Stadt, Vienna.

Klimt used symbolism as a means of describing ideas and states of mind without resorting to the more melodramatic devices of the Expressionists. In this case, the snake encircling the woman's neck sets the scene and the drawing of the hand which clasps it, and the raddled face, express the neurotic tension in a person consumed with envy of another's good fortune.

Portrait of a Woman in a Golden Dress (1886–87) Oil on panel. 46 x 26¹/₃in (117 x 67cm). Private collection.

The period when Klimt was using gold as a background or decorative element in his paintings was still in evidence when this picture of an unknown woman appeared. In his search for a new approach, he persuaded his brother Ernst and fellow painter Franz Matsch to collaborate with him in producing this picture, though where the contribution of each lay is not clear.

CHAPTER FOUR

THE SEARCH FOR TRUTH

Pregnant Woman with

Man (1903–04)

Chalk on paper. 17²/₃ x
12in (44.7 x 30.6cm).
Scottish National Gallery
of Modern Art, Edinburgh.

This naturalistic drawing
of a nude couple was a
study for a more dramatic
oil painting (*Hope I*,
1903), pages 86 and 87,
in which the woman
becomes the main

subject of the
composition, with her
bright red hair and a more
greatly distended belly.
The man is reduced to a
menacing dark shape in
the background where
there is also a skull. In
this way Klimt creates a
powerful symbolic
statement dealing with
the act of procreation and
the cycle of birth and
death.

The destruction of Klimt's high expectations for the
University Hall murals left him in a depressed mood.
The University had refused to annul his commission, or to
accept their money back, and he barricaded himself in his
studio where he kept the paintings which had yet to be
installed. It was not only the bureaucratic interference that
led to his retirement from the world, however. His own
artistic problems were also as much a valid reason. The new
direction of his art, demonstrated in the *Jurisprudence*
painting, was a venture into new ideas concerning painting
and he needed tranquillity in which to collect his thoughts.

Klimt's friendship with the Flöge family, especially
Emilie, was becoming indispensable to his peace of mind at
this point in his life and he now began to spend summers at

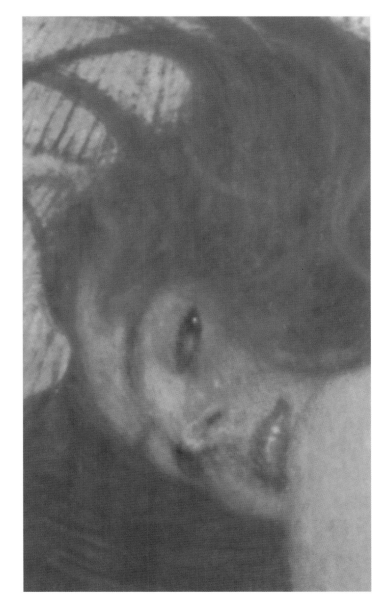

Goldfish (1901–02)
Oil on canvas. 71¼ x
26⅛in (181 x 66.5cm).
Kunstmuseum, Solothurn.

Fishes and mermaids
were frequently used by
Klimt at this period of his
development as symbols
of the new freedom in art
he was seeking. The nude
at the bottom of the
picture seems to have
upset his critics, however,
and Klimt, who was still
smarting from his
treatment by the
University authorities over
his murals, decided to
entitle the painting 'To my
critics'. Such bluntness
worried his friends who
considered this to be
politically unwise and he
reluctantly allowed himself
to be dissuaded from his
intention.

ABOVE

Here's a Kiss to the Whole World! (Detail from the Beethoven frieze, 1902)
Mixed media on stucco. 85 x 118in (216 x 300cm). Österreichische Galerie, Vienna.

When Klimt was asked to contribute a frieze to the Beethoven exhibition by his friend, Josef Hoffmann, he knew he had a free hand to do something original. The frieze was to go around a room which led to the giant statue of Beethoven by Klinger and was therefore going to attract public attention. Klimt used a variety of media, including gold leaf and mother-of-pearl, and various figures were introduced along the frieze, including a naked couple embracing in an example of Freudian symbolism.

OPPOSITE

The Knight (Detail from the Beethoven frieze, 1902)
Fresco. Österreichesche Galerie, Vienna.

The knight, reputed to be a portrait of Klimt's friend, the composer Gustav Mahler, is a symbol of heroism and Klimt used him not only to represent the spirit of the Secession but also the new approach to art and to life itself. It was a concept which was also common in other parts of Europe. In England the Pre-Raphaelites had taken the medieval world of knights and chivalry as themes for their paintings, and Tennyson's *Idylls of the Kings* (1859) was another example of the cult. Klimt's knight is portrayed in a stylized fashion as the artist moves ever further from realism.

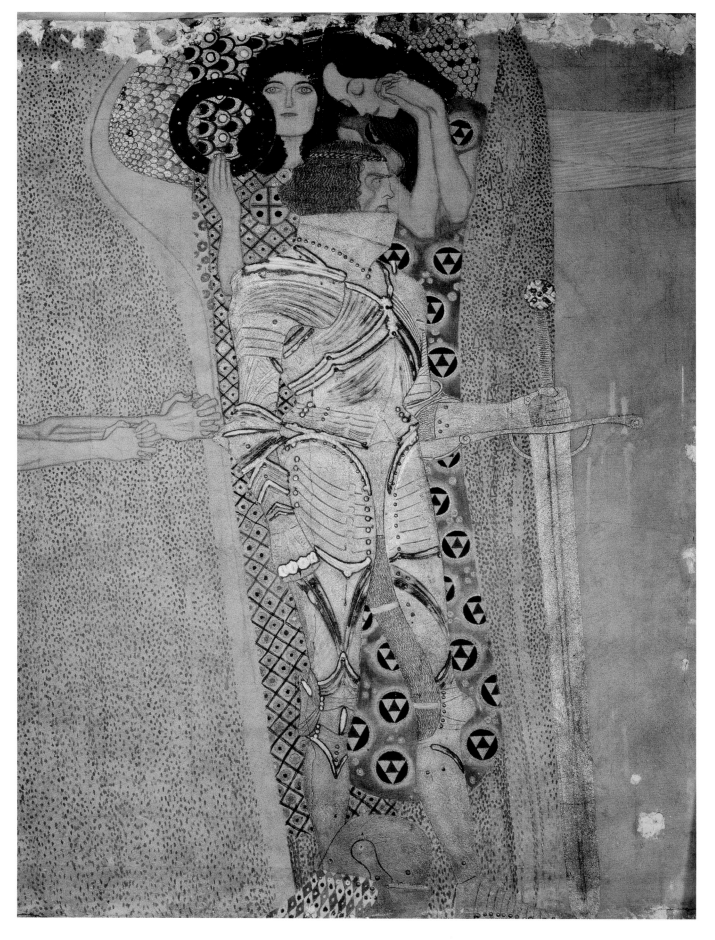

Hygieia (Detail of *Medecine*, 1900–07) Oil on canvas. Schloss Immendorf, Austria.

The University Hall murals, for which Klimt had been commissioned in the 1890s, had an unfortunate history. Believing that the project was one in which he could develop original ideas, Klimt put forward sketches which were

accepted but later rejected. His commission was to paint murals for three faculties, *Medecine*, *Jurisprudence* and *Philosophy*. Hygieia, the goddess of medecine, appears below a column of naked male and female bodies with the figure of death above them. This upset the faculty members because it suggested that medecine was impotent in the face of implacable mortality.

the Flöge country house on the Attersee, a small lake in the Salzkammergut. Here, he began to paint the landscapes that were to become an important feature of his work (p. 132).

The disagreements over the University Hall paintings rumbled on over a number of years during which Klimt was also involved in the Secession exhibitions. One of the most important of these took place in 1902, the exhibition being devoted to the theme of Beethoven and its centrepiece, a monumental statue of Beethoven in marble and bronze by the German sculptor Max Klinger. In honour of the composer and the sculpture the Secession building was remodelled and Secession members were invited to contribute appropriate paintings, sculptures and decorations. Klimt assumed responsibility for a frieze (p. 52) which was to run along the top of three walls at the entrance to the exhibition.

As the exhibition was a Secessionist one, where no commission from public authorities was involved, Klimt was

The Kiss (1907–08)
Mixed media. 71 x 71in
(180 x 180cm).
Österreichesches Galerie,
Vienna.

This version of *The Kiss*
was painted after Klimt
had used the theme in
the Beethoven frieze and
marks the climax of his
gold leaf period. The
affluent pre-First World
War Viennese lived a

somewhat raffish and
decadent life and the
gold, precious jewels and
other materials used in
the picture are an
appropriate indication of
their eagerness to display
their wealth.

able to work freely in the style which had aroused such criticism when he used it for his *Jurisprudence* painting. The frieze was conceived as a two-dimensional design using paint, gold and silver leaf, semi-precious stones, mirror glass and even nails. It was a *tour de force* in the new approach to painting for which Klimt was searching.

Its theme, according to the exhibition's catalogue, though not stated clearly enough, was the human longing for happiness. But its explanation was as perplexing as the work itself and appeared thus: 'The sufferings of feeble mankind; its appeal to the well-armed strong one as an external, and to compassion and ambition as internal forces motivating mankind to fight for happiness.'

Klimt declined to comment himself, but in the frieze is a warrior embellished with gold leaf, whom many believed to be modelled on Klimt's friend, Gustav Mahler (p.53), who conducted an arrangement of the theme from Beethoven's Fifth Symphony at the opening of the exhibition. Other personages in the frieze include naked women, dancers, an embracing couple and a monkey.

The Three Ages of Woman (1905)
Oil on canvas. 70 x 78in (178 x 198cm). Galleria Nazionale d'Arte Moderna, Rome.

There were several conflicting opinions concerning the nature of this work when it was exhibited at the Deutsche Künstlerbund Exhibition at Mannheim. Some of the adverse criticism may have been prompted by the subject, with its reminders of ageing and decay, but official reviewers limited their remarks to the technique which some found too geometrical.

The Golden Knight or
Life is a Struggle (1903)
Oil on canvas. 39^1/$_3$ x
39^1/$_3$in (100 x 100cm).
Private collection.

Knights in armour were
still popular icons at the
turn of the century and
Klimt used them as
symbols of hope, purity,
chivalry and gallantry,
virtues which he hoped
would have new meaning
in a society which was
rapidly changing. When
he painted *The Knight* (p.
53) for the Beethoven
frieze, his admiration for
the composer Gustav
Mahler was so great that
he is said to have painted
it in his image.

Visitors who flocked to the exhibition were shocked. The nudity seemed to have little to do with the great and serious master composer; one critic called it a show of artistic self-abuse, and another considered it to be more appropriate in a temple dedicated to Krafft-Ebing, the sexual psychopathologist. When the exhibition was over, the frieze was stored away by August Lederer and might well have been destroyed like Klimt's University Hall paintings: but enough of it remained for a discerning art lover to piece it together again. Thus a landmark in the work of the Austrian pioneer of Art Nouveau has been preserved and can be seen in the Secession building in Vienna.

Klimt was not a painter who felt the need to travel in order to study the works of the great masters or even to mingle with other artists in centres like Paris. Whether this was a lack of curiosity or simply a fear of travelling is not known, though his friend Carl Moll related that once, having arranged to meet him in Italy and failing to find him at the train platform barrier, he later discovered Klimt sitting on the departure platform, intending to take the next train back to Vienna.

Nevertheless, in 1903 Klimt decided to visit Ravenna. Once there, he immersed himself in a study of the Byzantine mosaics for which the Italian city is famous. The style of the mosaics, with their simplified drawings enclosed in glittering and colourful shards of stone and their flat unadorned backgrounds, struck a chord in Klimt. He recognized an affinity with his own concept of a decorated space which confirmed that his thinking was correct and which enabled him, once and for all, to discard the trappings of academic art and launch himself confidently into a new and personal style. It also strengthened his belief in one of the fundamental tenets of the Secession – that there was no dividing line between art and craft and that art was a means of expression accessible to everyone at all levels of understanding.

He was not alone in his ideas. An architect, Alfred Loos, and a writer, Karl Krauss, were also campaigning against the meretricious art and architecture of the Austrian Empire which they judged aimless and decadent. Joining the Secession, Kraus wrote an article for *Ver Sacrum* calling Vienna the 'Potemkin city' – a reference to the city of false façades built by General Potemkin to impress Catherine the

ABOVE

The dining room of Josef Hoffmann's Stoclet Palace, Brussels, built between 1905 and 1911, with a frieze designed by Gustav Klimt.

The role of the Klimt frieze in the Stoclet dining room can be well appreciated in this view of the entire room. Hoffmann's belief that all elements in a room should be integrated into the total design are well in evidence, with the curving arabesques of Klimt's frieze providing an appropriate contrast to the severity of the tables and chairs.

OPPOSITE

Detail of Gustav Klimt's frieze for the Stoclet Palace, showing the central portion based on a Tree of Life design.

In order to break the continuity of the frieze that ran around the Stoclet dining room, Klimt introduced abstract or symbolic forms intended to be decorative and quite different from the earlier Beethoven frieze. Here an ancient motif, the Tree of Life, has been used in which the leaves are triangles and the flowers circles.

Fulfilment (The Stoclet frieze, 1905–11) Tempera and watercolour. Österreichische Galerie, Vienna.

When his friend Josef Hoffmann asked Klimt to contribute to a palatial building he was creating for the coal magnate, Adolphe Stoclet, he was given a free hand to create a frieze for the dining room. Hoffmann was very much in

sympathy with the original ideas of the Secession, that art could also be applied to craftsmanship, and set out to produce a building that would embody this principle, even down to the cutlery and crockery used at table. Klimt chose The Tree of Life motif as his theme and executed it in an Art Nouveau manner apparent in the embracing couple seen here.

Great during the Russian empress's visit to the Crimea.

Alfred Loos wrote an article entitled 'Ornament and Crime', which argued that the buildings of the Ringstrasse were settings for a people only interested in pleasure, masked balls, gold-braided uniforms, bewigged waiters in breeches, and champagne and caviar. Klimt himself did not escape this acid criticism of Viennese society and his *Medicine* painting for the University Hall was described as 'a chaotic infusion of decrepit bodies which symbolically represent the conditions in the General Hospital'. Klimt was already moving towards the unpretentious simplicity which Loos and Krauss were promoting and which would later give rise to the concepts enshrined in the Bauhaus teaching in Germany.

By now, too, there were a growing number of art buyers who were prepared to support the new art. Among them was a Belgian industrialist and coal magnate called Adolphe Stoclet who commissioned the Vienna-trained architect Josef Hoffmann to build him a modern palace in Brussels. Hoffmann, who had designed the Beethoven exhibition and

OPPOSITE

Tree of Life with Shrub

(The Stoclet frieze,
1905–11).
Mixed media. 76¹/₃ x
46¹/₂in (194 x 118cm).
Österreichisches Galerie,
Vienna.

RIGHT

Study for Expectation

(The Stoclet frieze,
1905–11).
Mixed media. 76 x 45¹/₄in
(193 x 115cm).
Palais Stoclet, Brussels.

Although he was given a
free hand in creating the
ideas for the Stoclet
Palace decorations, Klimt
was obliged to preserve
the integrity of the total
design which his friend
Hoffmann demanded and
which led to every detail,
down to cutlery and
napkins, being regarded
as important parts of the
whole. However, this did
not prevent Klimt's
spectacular use of
abstract forms from
becoming a magnificent
decorative force.

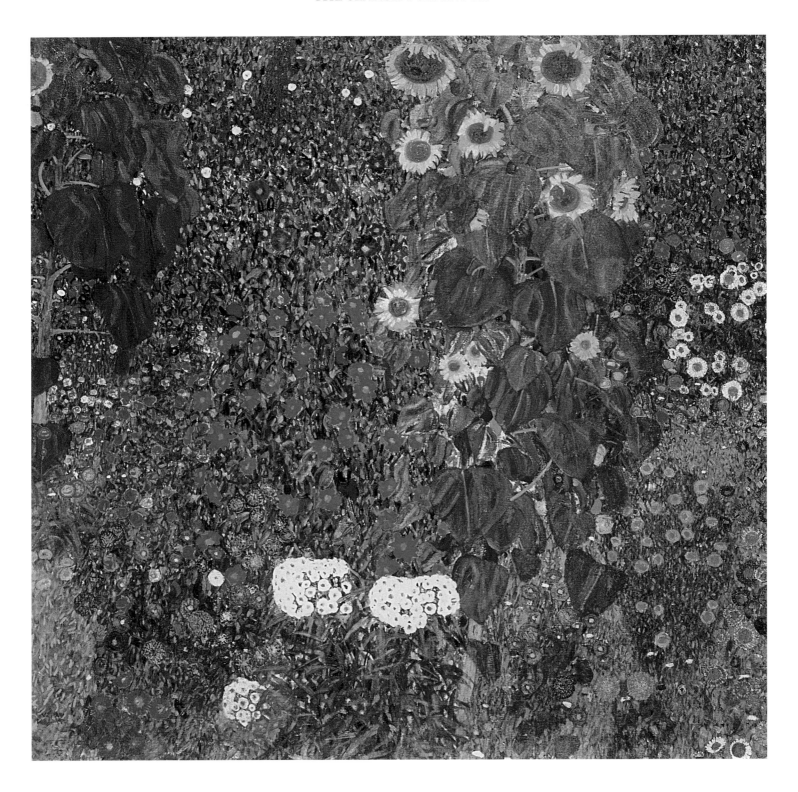

Farm Garden with Sunflowers (1905–06)
Oil on canvas.
43$\frac{1}{3}$ x 43$\frac{1}{3}$in (110 x 110cm).
Österreichisches Galerie, Vienna.

The sunflowers in Klimt's paintings do not exist alone but are part of organic nature and share the fate of all plant life. As such, they are not individual symbols but part of the overall pattern of life according to Klimt's philosophy. Klimt, like Monet, preferred gardens that seemed to evolve naturally rather than the orderly creations of man.

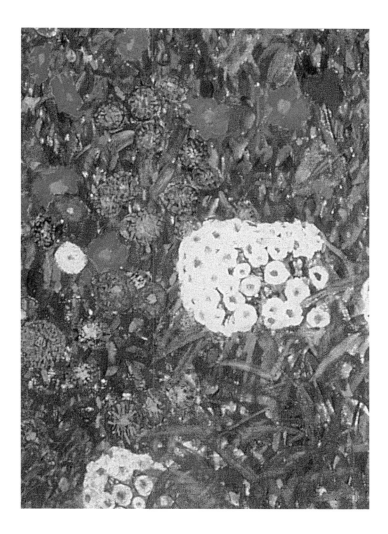

had worked with Klimt, sympathized with the Secessionist ideas of integrated art. In the Palais Stoclet, he was given a free hand to coordinate every aspect of the architecture, the decoration, the furniture and even the crockery and cutlery into the total design. Klimt and a number of Viennese craftsmen were to collaborate with Hoffmann on the Palais Stoclet for several years: the palace – fin de siècle Vienna transposed to pre-war Brussels – was to become known as an exemplar of the Art Nouveau style which, by 1911, the year it was completed, had become a design style popular throughout Europe.

Klimt's contribution to the Palais Stoclet was the decoration of the dining room (p. 62–67), consisting of nine panels, each approximately 6.6 x 3.3ft (2 x 1m) in size. He chose the Tree of Life as his theme and used a long spiral pattern spreading from its central trunk. This simple theme was expressed in an elaborate technique using paint, mosaics, glass and semi-precious stones. At one end was featured the figure called *Fulfilment* (p.64 and 65), which

Water Serpents I
(1904–07)
Watercolour and gold
paint on parchment. 19^{2}/$_{3}$
x 8in (50 x 20cm).
Österreichische Galerie,
Vienna.

Klimt's experiments with
various kinds of media,
which he had exploited to
the full in the Beethoven
frieze at the special 12th
Secession exhibition,
continued until he decided
to dedicate himself to
landscape painting and
began a serious study of
Impressionist techniques.
In this painting he is at his
most enthusiastic in his
use of mixed media and
uses watercolour, oil, gold
leaf, silver and other
materials to portray a
secret narcissistic world
of women in love with
one another.

for Klimt symbolized a love for the whole world, and which
he had already employed in the Beethoven frieze.

Klimt's frieze in the dining room of the Palais Stoclet
was the last of his mural works. He now began to
concentrate on landscapes, portraits of women and paintings
of symbolic expression in an Art Nouveau manner
resembling the *Jurisprudence* mural which had caused such
an uproar at the university.

The origins of Art Nouveau are obscure, but its curving,
sinuous lines and naturalistic forms suggest that it was
inspired by an instinctive social reaction to the advancing
tide of machinery and metal of the Industrial Revolution. In
England, the beginnings of the style were evident in the
work of the Pre-Raphaelite painters and of William Morris,

Danaë (1907–08)
Oil on canvas. 30¹/₃ x
32⁵/₈in (77 x 83cm).
Private Collection.

This daring composition,
depicting Zeus, the chief
of the Olympian gods,
entering Danaë disguised
as a shower of gold

coins, was not shown by
Klimt in the year that he
painted it, so he may
have had his doubts
regarding its reception in
a still overtly moral
society. Its circular
composition was typical
of other Klimt works of
the period such as The

Virgin (p. 78 and 79).
Surprisingly, however, he
did not use the square
canvas that had become
his favoured format and
which would have suited
the composition
admirably.

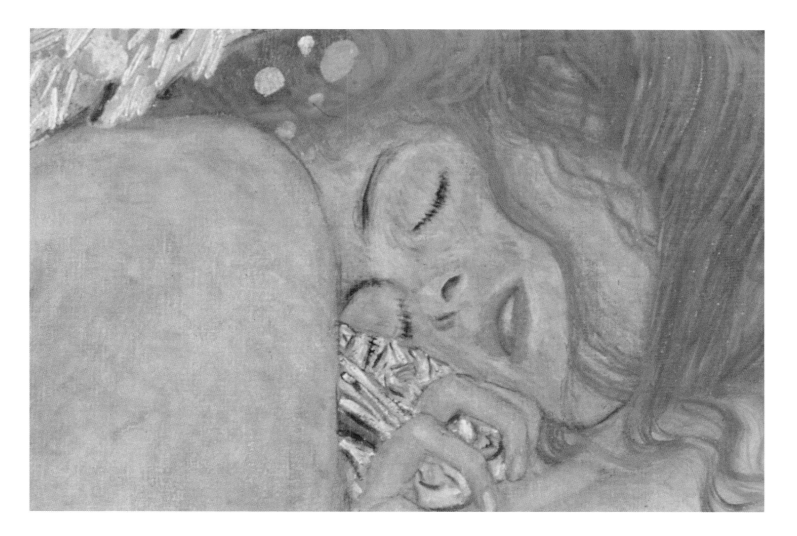

and it reached its apogee in the drawings of Aubrey
Beardsley. In Spain, the eccentric architect Antoní Gaudí was
creating the Sagrada Familia and other buildings in the style,
while in France Art Nouveau had permeated public buildings
and especially the Paris Métro: in New York Tiffany lamps
were hugely popular, and in Scotland the architect and
designer Charles Rennie Mackintosh was fighting entrenched
conservatism to introduce his own version of the Art
Nouveau style.

The style was destined for a rich, influential but short
life, cut off in its prime by the Great War and the destruction
of the sophisticated and affluent society which had come to
dominate the major countries of Europe and America. It
was, in a sense, the last dance of the romantic era which had
fired the imagination of artists of the 19th century. But its
death knell also announced a new wave of artists who were
severing their bonds from the past culture of Europe and
confirming their affinity with the new industrial world by
approaching nature as scientists under the banner of Cubism.

73

Judith II or **Salome**
(1909)
Oil on canvas. 70 x 18in
(178 x 46cm).
Museo d'Arte Moderna,
Venice.

The theme of Judith I (p. 41) is Judith holding the severed head of Holofernes. This version, Judith II, with its similar theme, could be more properly regarded as a portrait of Salome, which has a less noble theme in that she demanded the head of John the Baptist as a reward for dancing for her stepfather, Herod Antipas. The drawing of the face and hands of the dancer, with their rapacious appearance, verge on Expressionism, though the severe hard-edged drawing dulls the emotional edge.

When Klimt conceived his decorations for the Palais Stoclet in 1904, Picasso was about to stun the world with his painting, *Les Demoiselles d'Avignon*, the forerunner of Cubism. But Picasso and Cubism made little impact on the Viennese art world, which still looked to the past for ideas on what constituted the good life and popular culture for all. Even if he had known of the innovations Picasso was achieving in Paris, there would have been little impact on Klimt. His struggle to modernize art in Vienna was still based on simplicity and elegance; the harsh truth that the Cubists sought was not in his nature.

In the symbolic paintings, figures of women predominated, as in *Water Serpents I* (p. 70 and 71), started in 1904. In this work, Klimt gives full rein to his experiments with multi-media techniques and uses gouache, watercolour, gold leaf, silver and semi-precious stones which, as well as providing new means of expression, had a direct public appeal and added value irrespective of the aesthetic merits of the work. In 1907, *Water Serpents* came to be valued at 5000 guilders.

A more sombre subject was *The Three Ages of Women* (p. 58–59) in which Klimt divides the simple background for the painting into two horizontal spaces, before which he places the dominant figure of an old woman, shoulders bent,

Death and Life (c.1911)
Oil on canvas. 70 x 78in
(178 x 198cm).
Private Collection.

Klimt had a morbid streak
in his nature, evidence of
which began to appear
more insistently in his
later work. This expressed
the underlying decadence
and disenchantment that
lay beneath the waltz
society of Vienna and the
growing anxiety regarding
the true significance of
life, following the
revelations of Darwin and
Freud. The agglomeration
of bodies into the solid
block of the design was a
Klimt characteristic, used
since the turn of the
century.

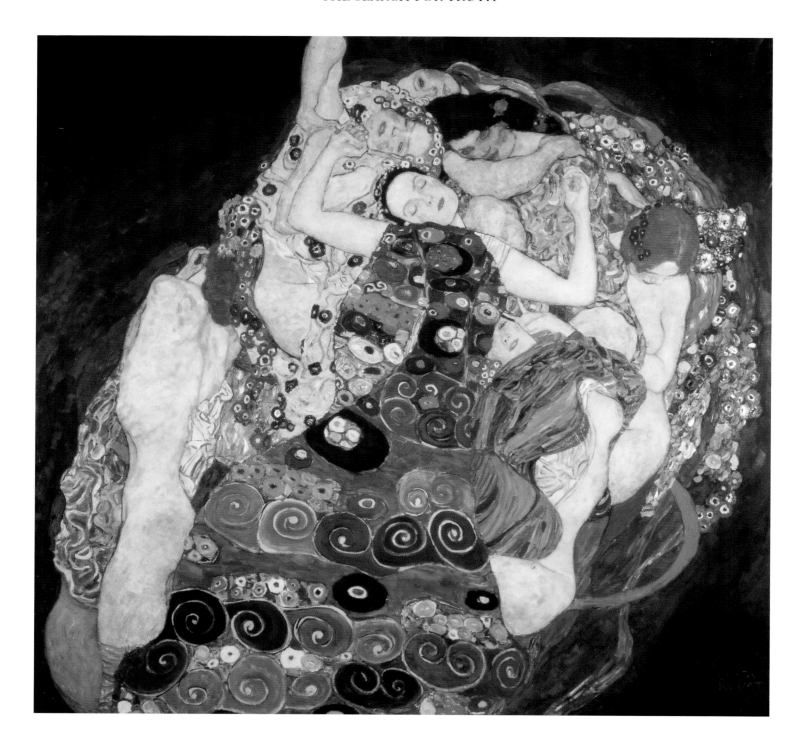

The Virgin (1913)
Oil on canvas. 75 x 79in
(190 x 200cm).
Národní Gallery, Prague.

Also called *The Maiden,*
this large painting is one
of Klimt's symbolic
works, though the
symbolism is a little
obscure. There appear to
be seven females in a
circular composition
embedded in a quilt of

coloured patches. Klimt
liked to have nude
models walking about,
not posed, in his studio
and the painting may
have been simply the
reaction to seeing his
models resting on a
divan. Klimt saw the

female as the life spirit
and the meaning intended
here may be the same as
that of traditional
paintings such as *La
Source* by Ingres.

head inclined and belly protruding. At a slightly lower level, and set against a decorative column that holds all the figures together, is a young woman and child. The decorative swathe at the woman's knees suggests a skull – whether by accident or design; but it is a hint of the symbolism that Klimt linked to his decorative style and which added a more profound meaning to mere design.

Klimt was reluctant to exhibit his symbolic work so soon after the wave of criticism of his University Hall murals. His painting, *Hope I* (p. 86 and 87), in which a very pregnant red-haired woman stands in profile staring at the viewer, while in the background looms a dark shape with a death's head skull, was not exhibited until 1907.

This was the year that Klimt painted one of his most famous and suggestive, some say pornographic, paintings, *Danaë* (p. 72 and 73). The raised thigh of the curled-up figure of the young woman, with the god Zeus entering her disguised as a shower of gold coins, makes a strikingly erotic composition and marked a moment of change in Klimt's work. After this date, his use of gold leaf declined under the impact of Impressionist influences, as did his ventures into symbolist painting. In 1908, the work of Vincent Van Gogh also began to appear in Vienna and provided Klimt with food for thought concerning his own landscapes.

When the Archduke Franz Ferdinand, the heir to the Austrian throne, was assassinated at Sarajevo in 1914, Klimt,

Adam and Eve (1917–18)
Oil on canvas. 68 x 24in (173 x 60cm). Österreichische Galerie, Vienna.

As in his painting *Hope I* (p. 86 and 87), Klimt has placed the man as a dark, almost indistinguishable shape in the background.

This was one of Klimt's last paintings and the idea that woman is the source and mistress of life, which he had held throughout his career, emerges strongly. His pantheistic philosophy also accounts for his dedication to nature and landscape painting.

like all citizens of the Austro-Hungarian Empire, was deeply affected. This was an ominous time for the new Austria which had been evolving so optimistically and successfully from the old rigidities of Empire. The Great War brought many privations to Austria, as well as hordes of refugees and wounded soldiers, and it seemed that the gaiety of Viennese society had a short span to run. Then the death of the Emperor Franz Joseph in 1916 spelt the end of an era and Austria's future seemed uncertain indeed.

There was little that Klimt could do. One of his friends and students, Oskar Kokoschka, volunteered and was wounded; another, Egon Schiele, already depressed and neurotic and obsessed by Freudian symbolism, was soon to die. Klimt turned again to symbolism to express the feelings that he usually kept hidden. In 1915 he began a picture that he called *Death and Life* (p. 76 and 77), in which a decorative column contains the figure of Death, while facing it is a mass of intertwined figures against a dark background.

This dark mood only partially dominated Klimt's thoughts, however. In 1915, he also painted two rather more optimistic and defiant pictures. One, *Adam and Eve* (left and opposite), includes a naked young woman exuding fertility and vitality. The other, *Baby*, possesses an exuberance of colourful decorative design which seems to symbolize the potency of life which had motivated Klimt since his break with established art. Both paintings remained unfinished at the time of Klimt's death in February, 1918.

CHAPTER FIVE
KLIMT'S WOMEN

Klimt's paintings of women, many containing erotic overtones; his relationship with a model, Mizzi Zimmerman, who sued him for the maintenance of their child; allegations that he had at least a dozen mistresses; his lifelong friendship with his sister-in-law, Emilie Flöge – all served to suggest of a man of complex character, at least where his relationships with women were concerned.

He was no ordinary bohemian artist, rather a product of the rigid social culture spawned by the Austro-Hungarian Empire, a male-oriented society where women were regarded either as delicate untouchables or as easily available servants and shopgirls. He was also a man with strong family bonds and his close relationship with his mentally unstable mother undoubtedly raised fears in his own mind and was probably the cause of his hypochondria. He maintained a good relationship with his sisters, Johanna and Hermine, who later remembered him as a normal boy with a good appetite, especially for dumplings, and fond of animals.

Yet this normal young man never married nor, its seems, ever had a long-lasting attachment to another woman, except for Emilie Flöge, though his relationship with her appears to have been close, but platonic. Being a man who preferred to keep his private thoughts to himself, who seldom wrote

Portrait of Serena Lederer (1899)
Oil in canvas. 74 x 34in (188 x 85.4cm). The Metropolitan Museum of Art, New York.

The beautiful Serena Lederer was the wife of August Lederer, one of Klimt's most enthusiastic patrons. The artist has painted her in a highly romantic manner, concentrating on her splendid head of hair and expressive face and allowing her white dress to almost merge into the background.

Portrait of Hermine Gallia (1904)
Oil on canvas. 67 x 38in (170 x 96cm). The National Gallery, London.

This is possibly not as adventurous a portrait as many of Klimt's others and it is possible that its relative dullness may be due to the passage of time. However, it is still in a romantic style, and marks a boundary between Klimt's Impressionist technique and the abstract patterning of his later portraits. A hint of things to come can be glimpsed in the skirt of the dress where Klimt has introduced some unusual shapes.

Emilie Flöge (1902)
Oil on canvas. 71¼ x 33in
(181 x 84cm).
Historisches Museum der
Stadt, Vienna.

Klimt spent nearly all his
holidays at the Flöges'
lakeside house on the
Attersee and was
welcomed there as one of
the family. Emilie and her
sister ran a fashion shop
in Vienna and Klimt often
helped them out with
new ideas for dresses,
which were loose-fitting
and informal. Klimt and
Emilie had become very
close friends after her
husband, Klimt's brother,
died, though there is little
evidence to suggest that
they were lovers.

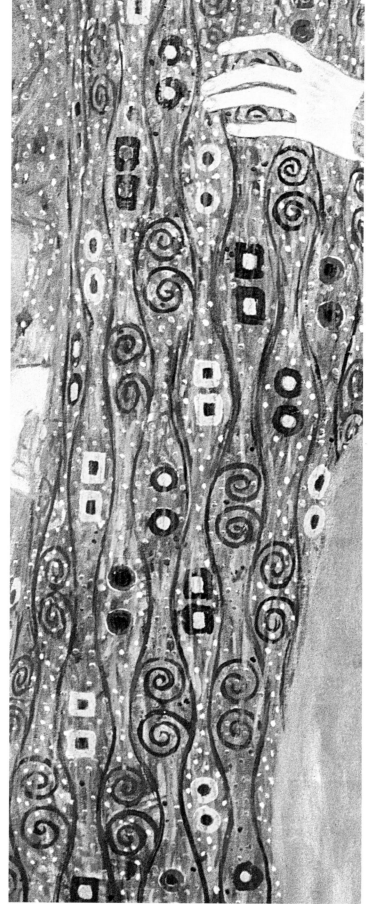

Hope I (1903)
Oil in canvas. 71¹/₄ x
26³/₈in (181 x 67cm).
National Gallery of
Canada, Ottawa.

This is the first of two
versions, the second
being *Hope II* (p. 92 and
93). *Hope I* was judged
the more shocking for the
total nudity of the subject
and the prominent
position of a skull in the
background together with

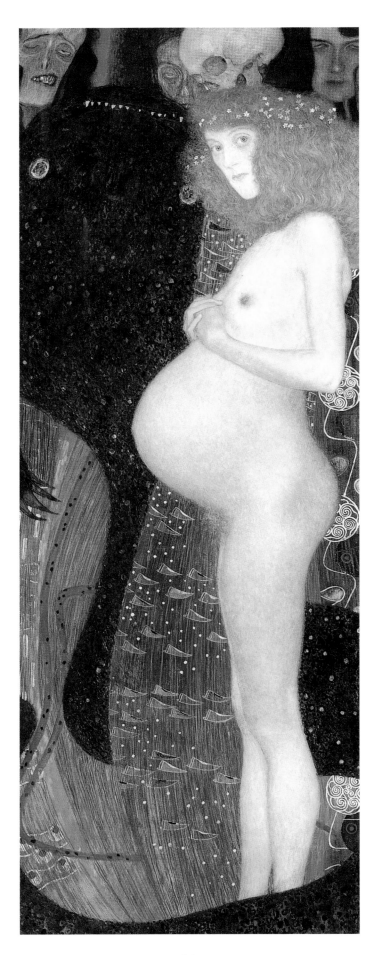

a dark figure of a man.
Hope II, however, has a
rather more covered up
appearance and is more
decorative in treatment.
The morbid streak that
ran through much of
Klimt's work can be
traced back to his youth
spent with an unstable
mother and his fears for
his own mental stability,
though he developed no
actual symptoms of
mental disorder.

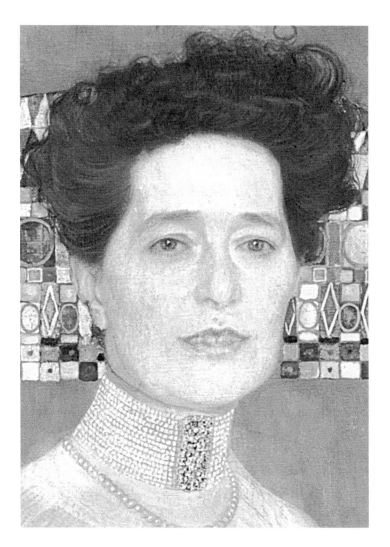

Portrait of Fritza Riedler
(1906)
Oil on canvas. 60¼ x
52⅜ (153 x 133cm).
Österreichisches Galerie,
Vienna.

This fine portrait in Klimt's
elegant Art Nouveau style
was one of many that he
produced for fashionable
Viennese women, at a
time that he was also
developing his symbolic
paintings. The
composition, with its
ample spaces, is
reminiscent of the

Japanese prints which
had become popular in
Europe. They were a
source of inspiration to
the Impressionists and
artists, such as Degas,
providing them with the
impetus to embrace new
ideas concerning
composition. However,
the reactionary nature of
the Austrian
Establishment had had
the effect of delaying the
arrival of new ideas in
Vienna.

personal letters and did not keep a journal, Klimt's attitude
to women is probably best sought in his paintings, which he
always claimed said everything that could be said on the
subject.

His earliest paintings of women were conventional
classical nudes, as in his theatre murals. In 1898, however,
two paintings by Klimt indicated new directions, both in
style and content. The portrait of Sonja Knips (p. 34), a
young woman who frequented Viennese artistic circles,
indictes that Klimt was moving towards an Impressionist
technique. The sitter's light pink dress, delicately painted
using long brushstrokes, merges gently into a dark
background. Around Sonja's head there is a suggestion of
flowers and the diagonal composition appears to be derived
from the same Japanese art that had influenced the
Impressionists' concept of composition. It is an attractive
portrait of a young woman.

The second 1898 painting of a woman reveals Klimt's

Portrait of Margaret Stonborough-Wittgenstein (1905)
Oil on canvas. 71 x 35³⁄₈in (180 x 90cm). Neue Pinakothek, Munich.

The handsome woman that Klimt has placed against an abstract background, which he added after completing the portrait, is Margaret Wittgenstein, the mother of the celebrated philosopher and scientist who argued that statements were only working symbols of truths for which there was no language and which were therefore inexpressible

developing interest in symbolism expressed through the female figure. The painting is of Minerva or Pallas Athene (p. 38), the goddess whom the Secession artists saw as their patron. Klimt portrays her with a golden helmet and gives her a breastplate of gold coins on which is superimposed a head of Medusa and a standing naked woman. Athene is a woman seen by Klimt as a personification of power and authority, an icon and symbol of qualities which Klimt regarded as facets of womanhood. In the coming years, Klimt was to develop the two views of women these paintings expressed.

When painting portraits of women, Klimt observed the social norms and preserved a discreet distance between himself and his sitters, avoiding any familiarity which might be misconstrued. On one occasion, however, he may have been indiscreet, for gossip accused him of the attempted seduction of Alma Schindler, the stepdaughter of his painter friend Carl Moll. Klimt replied promptly and energetically to the accusation in a letter to Moll.

'I came to your house innocently,' he wrote. 'Alma appealed to me simply in the way that a beautiful child appeals to a painter. I never courted her in the proper sense of the word.' The matter ended there and Klimt and Moll remained friends. Alma later married the composer Gustav Mahler, but left him for the architect Walter Gropius; Mahler was compelled to look to the services of Sigmund Freud to restore his peace of mind.

Hope II (1907–08)
Oil on canvas. $43^1/_3$ x
$43^1/_3$in (110 x 110cm).
The Museum of Modern
Art, New York.

The abstract patterning,
which Klimt had
experimented with on the
dress of the portrait of his
sister-in-law, Emilie Flöge
(p. 84), later developed
into a device by which he
could express his deep
feelings on the unity of
life with art. In the single
shapes which make up
the whole, Klimt has
embedded symbolic
forms and figures to
suggest the beginnings of
a new life.

Portrait of Adele Bloch-Bauer I (1907)
Oil and gold on canvas
54⅓ x 54⅓in (138 x 138cm). Österreichische Galerie, Vienna.

Adele was the wife of a rich industrialist, Ferdinand Bloch-Bauer, and she is also reputed to have been Klimt's mistress. The painting is a rich combination of naturalism and abstract forms, reminiscent of motifs occurring in ancient Egyptian artefacts in which Klimt was undoubtedly interested. These may also have inspired the spandrels for the Kunsthistorisches Museum, Vienna (p. 20–21) and the Tree of Life motif of the Stoclet Palace frieze (p. 62–67). (See also a further portrait of Adele Bloch-Bauer on p. 102.)

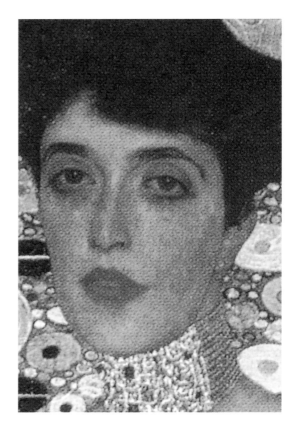

In 1899, Klimt painted a portrait of Serena Lederer (p. 82), the wife of the wealthy distiller, August Lederer, in which he poses her standing in a white dress which merges with the background, the intention being to emphasize Serena's black hair and lustrous dark eyes. Her husband was so pleased with the painting that he gave Klimt 35,000 crowns for it and became one of his most enthusiastic patrons. Sadly, Lederer's fine collection of art was destroyed by retreating German troops in 1945.

Though he had lost commissions from public bodies as a result of his disagreement over the University Hall paintings, Klimt was now much in demand privately and from now on portraits of women prominent in society would feature regularly in his work. Among the most memorable of such paintings were those of Margaret Stonborough-Wittgenstein (p. 90), wife of the magnate Wittgenstein and mother of Ludwig Wittgenstein, the philosopher; Charlotte Pollitzer; Friederike Maria Beer, daughter of an entertainments entrepreneur, whose portrait was also painted by Egon Schiele; Eugenia Primavesi, wife of a well-known art dealer; and Adele Bloch-Bauer, wife of an ex-officer in the Imperial army, who became Klimt's mistress. Adele Bloch-Bauer

Lady with Hat and Feather Boa (1909)
27¹/₈ x 21²/₃in (69 x 55cm). Österreichische Galerie, Vienna.

Klimt produced a few uncommissioned paintings of unidentified women which as a rule were simpler in form and were of women such as this – attractive, vivacious and wearing big hats, furs or muffs, as in *The Black Feathered Hat* (1910). In producing these paintings he was freeing himself from the tyranny of producing portraits of actual people and the need to flatter them by reproducing all the trappings of their wealth and power. Klimt probably saw this as a welcome change.

(p. 94 and 95), painted in a superb example of Klimt's 'golden' period in 1907, was also the model for his celebrated 1901 painting, *Judith I* (p. 40 and 41), in which Judith is clearly portrayed as a femme fatale.

Klimt's personal style of portraiture reached its peak in his 1902 portrait of Emilie Flöge (p. 84 and 85). Emilie had become a fashionable dress designer with a shop in the Ringstrasse and had asked Klimt to design some dresses for her in the new loose and unconstricted style which did not require women to be enclosed in corsets and other restraining undergarments. He painted her in one of her own dresses, giving her an attenuated Mannerist appearance and making a feature of the material of the dress, the strong abstract pattern of which was extended by Klimt into an upstanding frame for her head. The effect of the strong patterning against a flat background was to become a device which gave Klimt's paintings an uniquely personal decorative style.

RIGHT

**Seated Woman with
Fur Wrap and
Headdress** (1917–18)
Pencil on paper. 22³/₈ x
14³/₄in (56.8 x 37.5cm).
Private collection.

Like most artists, Klimt's
response to something
which interested him was
to draw a quick sketch to
remind him of what he
was seeing. In this case,
the subject may have
been a friend or someone
who instantly appealed to
him on account of her
fashionable appearance.

OPPOSITE

**Portrait of Mäda
Primavesi** (1912)
Oil on canvas. 59 x
43¹/₃in (150 x 110cm).
The Metropolitan
Museum of Art, New
York.

The daughter of Otto
Primavesi, the financier of
the Vienna Workshop –
the establishment created
after the Secession to
further the movement for
unified arts and crafts –
was a young girl poised
between childhood and
adolescence when Klimt
painted her. He has made
her look older and more
sophisticated, and the
short white dress is a
foretaste of the style of
the 1920s. Other
elements of the picture,
however, are distinctly
oriental.

Klimt's portrait work and his symbolist paintings
eventually began to converge in terms of technique and
appearance. In his 1906 portrait of Fritza Riedler (p. 88 and
89), the Impressionistic atmosphere of earlier portraits has
disappeared and the square canvas is filled with rectangular
shapes positioned behind the subject, who is seated on a
boldly patterned armchair set against a pinkish-red
background. In the great 1907 portrait of Adele Bloch-
Bauer (p. 94 and 95), extensive use is made of gold
patterning set against a golden background with only the
head, shoulders and arms of the black-haired sitter creating a
strong focal point.

Women Friends
(1916–17)
Oil on canvas. 39 x 39in
(99 x 99cm).
Österreichisches Galerie,
Vienna.

August Lederer was a collector and sponsor of much of Klimt's work and this painting was destroyed with others for the University Hall when, in 1945, retreating German troops set fire to his country home which housed the collection. However, studies and photographs remain as examples of the lost works. This was one of Klimt's last paintings and shows two women who may or may not have been lovers, though the title is ambiguous.

Adele Bloch-Bauer II
(1912)
Oil on canvas. 75 x 47¼in
(190 x 120cm).
Österreichische Galerie,
Vienna.

When he made this
painting, Klimt had largely
abandoned the elaborately
decorative abstract
patterning and use of gold
paint of the earlier Bloch-
Bauer portrait of 1907
(p. 94 and 95). The
change of style is marked:
although there is still a
high degree of decoration,
it is not as artificial and
the personality of the
subject is allowed to
shine through. Klimt was
now immersed in painting
landscapes and was
seeking a simpler form of
expression possessing a
deeper emotional content.

Portrait of a Lady

(1917–18)

Oil on canvas. 71 x
35½in (180 x 90cm).
Neue Galerie der Stadt,
Linz.

This unfinished picture of
Maria Monk clearly
shows how Klimt planned
his decorative portraits.
The drawing is tentative,
leaving room for
alterations before the
forms of the design are
finally resolved. However,
the head is from the start
firmly stated in order to
identify the subject.

OPPOSITE
Seated Woman (1908)
Pencil and crayon. 22 x
13in (56 x 33cm).
Private collection

Klimt's drawing had
become more precise by
the time he sketched this
figure. There is nothing
tentative in the line
describing the seated
figure which was an
inspiration to Egon
Schiele, a Klimt student,
who became a master of
line drawing, albeit with a
more bitterly emotional
content.

ABOVE
Seated Girl In Shadow
Pencil on paper. 17½ x
12½in (44.5 x 31.8cm).
Private Collection.

Klimt's line drawings
were rarely hard-edged
but had a searching
quality about them rather
than an intention to make
a positive statement. This
gives them a feeling of
atmosphere and space
and is the approach of a
painter rather than a
draughtsman.

ABOVE
Standing Robed Woman
(c. 1916)
Pencil on paper. 21 x
13¾in (53.3 x 35cm).
Private Collection.

Klimt made drawings for
two reasons, either as
preliminary studies for
finished paintings or as
drawings, usually erotic,
intended to stand in their
own right. This may well
be a preparation for a
future portrait though
whether or not it was
realized is not certain.

CHAPTER SIX
THE NUDE DRAWINGS

Klimt's relationships with women appear to have been rather ambiguous. He was certainly fond of them and liked having several naked models in his studio at one time, engaged in the normal everyday activities of companions sharing a living space: reading, sleeping, cooking, dressing and undressing and attending to their toilettes.

Klimt enjoyed looking at them, noting the way they moved, their mannerisms as well as their idiosyncracies, but his drawings of them give little insight into their emotional lives or his own feelings towards them. He undoubtedly had an occasional sexual relationship and, in one case, provided financial support for an illegitimate child. However, he was a reserved man not given to communicating his private thoughts either in journals, diaries, or letters to his friends, so there is little to be known of his private life.

The Viennese society of his youth was, as in most parts of the world at that time, a male-dominated one, and Klimt, being a product of that society, was no different to his contemporaries. His feelings towards women were very mixed: there were the goddesses on the one hand, usually from the upper stratas of society, who were regarded as unattainable and there to be worshipped, while on the other was the far more accessible world of shopgirls, servants, models and, of course, prostitutes.

When one looks at Klimt's female nudes, they are sensitive though impersonal. There is none of the erotic energy or neurotic tension that features in the work of his pupil, Egon Schiele, neither have they the pantheistic earth-mother quality of Oskar Kokoschka's women. If anything, they resemble spoilt, indulged pets, stretched out langourously in sleep, curled up in meditative poses, or insouciantly dressing or undressing.

Klimt seems to have had a Rousseauesque vision of the world as a Garden of Eden, rather as Gauguin yearned for the South Sea islands. It was a common fantasy of the times: an unspoilt world full of unspoilt people living the innocent lives of Adam and Eve before they encountered the serpent. In the end, Klimt turned from people to landscapes, finding in them the purity and depth of meaning for which he had ben searching since he decided to desert the safe, predetermined world of academicism and search for other ways.

ABOVE

Reclining Woman

(c.1914)

Pencil on paper. 14^1/$_2$ x
22in (37 x 56cm).
Private collection.

Klimt has caught an
unguarded moment of
happy relaxation in the
studio as his model
stretches out on a divan,
her robe open to reveal
her attractive body.

LEFT

Seated Woman (1916)

Pencil on Japan paper.
22 x 14^1/$_2$in (56 x 37cm).
Private collection.

This frontal view of a
seated model has drawn
an erotic response from
Klimt, but like most
artists he has chosen to
sublimate it in order to
focus on the drawing
itself. The effect of pencil
on soft paper gives
another dimension to a
flat line drawing.

GVSTAV
KLIMT
NACHLASS

OPPOSITE TOP

Nude Woman in Bed

(c.1914)

Pencil on paper. 14¹/₂ x
22¹/₂in (37 x 57.2cm).
Private collection.

The raised leg suggests
that relaxation is not total
and that the pose is not a
natural one for a woman
on the verge of sleep.

OPPOSITE BELOW

Couple in Bed (c.1915)
Pencil on paper. 14¹/₂ x
22in (37 x 56cm).
Private collection.

Clothes have been pulled
up to reveal the man's
haunches; but the sexual
relationship between the
two has not been
stressed and they seem
more like loving
companions than lustful
lovers.

RIGHT

**Woman with Bloomers
Looking to the Left**

(c.1916)
Pencil and coloured
crayons on paper. 22¹/₂ x
14¹/₂in (57.2 x 37cm).
Private collection.

The woman seems to be
chagrined by her sudden
exposure. This is unusual,
as Klimt did not often
portray strong emotions.

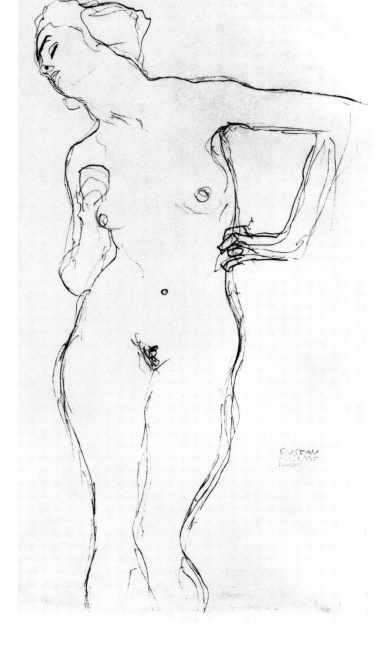

OPPOSITE

Seated Woman (c.1917)
Pencil on paper. 22 x
14³/₈in (56 x 36.5cm).
Private collection.

The model has been
drawn from a low angle
which revels a glimpse of
pubic hair. Such realism
had been regarded as
indecent, even up to the
time of Modigliani, when
a show of his nude
paintings, exhibited in
Paris, were forciby
removed by the police.

ABOVE

Young Woman (1917)
Pencil on paper. 22¹/₈ x
14⁵/₈ in (56.2 x 37.2cm).
Private collection.

Since the time of the
Greeks, a semi-clothed
woman has been
regarded as more erotic
than a clothed one, for
something half revealed
preserves its mystery.
Klimt enjoyed the
company of women and
regarded them as
symbols of life itself.

ABOVE

Nude (1917)
Pencil on paper. 14¹/₂ x
21³/₄inm (37 x 55.2cm).
Private collection.

This woman could well
be drying her back after
taking a bath, the kind of
transient moment Degas
liked to capture and

which can be seen in his
series of pictures of
women bathing and
attending to their
toilettes. Klimt has caught
the tilt of the head and
the sinuous movement of
the body with acute
perception.

OPPOSITE TOP
Two Women Asleep
Pencil on paper.
Private collection.

The sight of two women
resting or sleeping
together was not unusual
in Klimt's studio and did
not necessarily suggest a
sexual bond. Klimt
regarded nudity as
perfectly natural and he
would not have given any
particular emphasis to
such a situation.

OPPOSITE BELOW
Sleeping Nude (c.1916)
Pencil and coloured
crayons on paper. $13^5/_8$ x
$21^5/_8$in (34.5 x 54.4cm).
Private collection.

This is a model bored or
fatigued after a long
session posing for an
artist who is too absorbed
in his work to be sociable.

RIGHT
**Standing Nude, Girl
Looking Up**
Charcoal on brown paper.
$17^1/_2$ x $12^1/_2$in (44.5 x
31.8cm). Private
collection.

From a low viewpoint,
Klimt has emphasized the
woman's belly and
buttocks, describing two
sensual curves.

CHAPTER SEVEN

THE
LANDSCAPES

Klimt turned to landscape painting late in his career and after the foundation of the Vienna Secessionist group in 1897. This was the watershed of his life as a painter, a point undoubtedly reached as a result of his disappointment and irritation at the rejection of his murals by the Commission of the Ministry of Education responsible for the artistic affairs of the University of Vienna.

As a decorator of public buildings, Klimt had suffered for years from the pronouncements of a philistine bureaucracy whose philosophy of art was based on the principle of repeating what had gone before because it was considered acceptable to the people who mattered.

In his University Hall panels, especially *Jurisprudence*, Klimt had attempted to escape from old formulas to find a

OPPOSITE
Beech Forest I (c. 1902)
Oil on canvas. 39$^{1/3}$ x
39$^{1/3}$in (100 x 100cm).
Gemäldegalerie Neue
Meister, Dresden.

The closely planted trees
with their mottled trunks
create an enclosed space
that appealed to Klimt in
his later work and
suggested a microcosm
of nature within a greater
macrocosm of infinite
space, which Klimt has
emphasized with
glimpses of sky seen
through the trees.

RIGHT
**After the Rain: Garden
with Chickens in St
Agatha** (1899)
Oil on canvas. 31$^{1/2}$ x
15$^{3/4}$in (80 x 40cm).
Österreichische Galerie,
Vienna.

This was painted in upper
Austria as Klimt was
working on the University
Hall murals and provided
a welcome relief from his
dealings with University
officialdom. The
introduction of chickens
into a painting is unusual
though the motif was
later repeated in *Garden
Path with Chickens* (p.
129).

Farmhouse with Birch Trees (1900)
Oil on canvas. 31$\frac{1}{2}$ x 31$\frac{1}{2}$in (80 x 80cm). Österreichische Galerie, Vienna.

Although Klimt did not take to the colour theories of the Impressionists, either because he did not care to, or did not fully understand them, he adopted the technique of short brushstrokes and open compositions with large empty foregrounds, found in Monet's work. Here, Klimt has made an entire picture from a field with a few silver birches, the farmhouse appearing only as a small strip on the horizon.

way of expressing philosophical ideas through symbolism. The failure of his attempt to communicate ideas in a new way had left him angry but not discouraged. Although he had never been a militant member of artists' groups and was an introverted and diffident man, Klimt had allowed himself to be elected president of the Secessionists. Thus he became a prime mover in the striving of the Viennese artists towards modernity. But underneath the calm surface of Klimt's public persona, his mind was in ferment.

The end of the 19th century was a time of intellectual and social upheaval in Europe, the effects of which were felt even in the staid and reactionary society of the Austro-Hungarian Empire. The theories of Darwin, Freud, Nietsche and Marx, among others, were causing a re-assessment of past beliefs and what had once seemed permanent and inviolate was beginning to be questioned.

Klimt, like everyone around him, had in his youth accepted a positivist view of life in which progress was in the nature of things and change was a gradual process that did not upset the structure of life. Now, he began to have second thoughts, the continuing contact with new influences leading him to question the significance of his own work.

Like Gauguin at Pont Aven, he had begun to ask the questions which Gauguin had made the title of one of his works: Where do we come from? Who are we ? Where are we going? – questions which the Church and State, which had always supplied people with answers, preferred not to be asked.

Roses under the Trees
(1905)
Oil on canvas. 43¹⁄₃ x
43¹⁄₃in (110 x 110cm).
Musée d'Orsay, Paris.

This painting, which once belonged to the Zuckerandel Collection in Vienna, can no longer be traced and may have been the victim of anti-Semitic persecution or lost during the First World War. Klimt has skilfully contrasted the luxuriant vegetative life of a tree with the delicate but similar vitality of a rose bush, which climbs ever upwards to meet its host's overhanging branches.

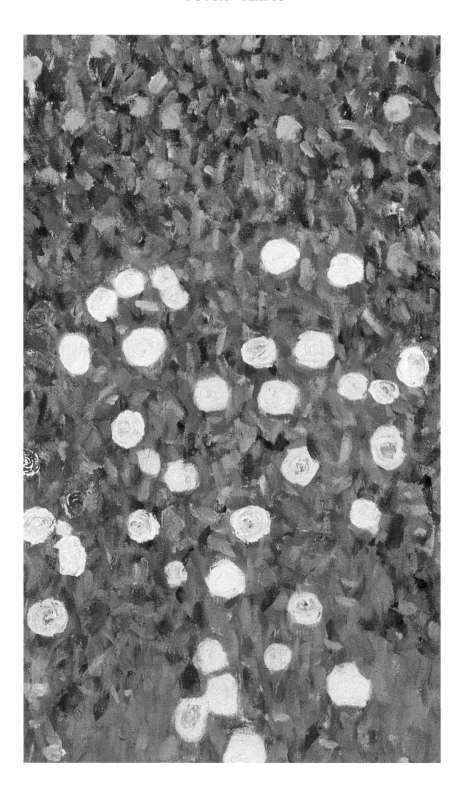

Another influence at work in Klimt's mind can be traced to the effect of the Secessionists, who had pressed for the acceptance of the work of artists from other countries by galleries and museums in Vienna. This departure from a previously isolationist attitude brought Klimt face to face with the work of Claude Monet and the Impressionists.

Monet had become a leading exponent of the genre and by experimenting with painting in the open air had experienced the startling effects of light and shade on natural objects more usually painted in the conventional manner in a studio. Trees, shrubs, water ceased to be gloomy objects on treacly canvases and became part of a shimmering, moving experience of the landscape itself, constantly transformed by the ever-changing fluctuations of light.

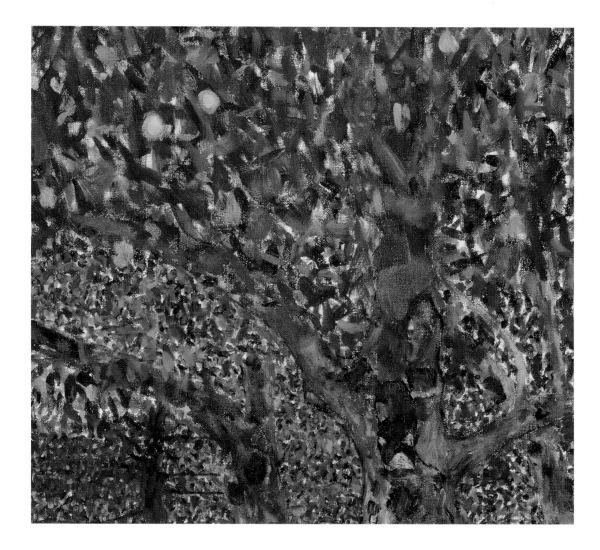

The Pear Tree (1903)
Oil and casein on canvas.
39³/₄ x 39³/₄in (101 x
101cm). Busch-Reisinger
Museum, Harvard
University, Cambridge,
Mass.

In his efforts to identify with
nature, Klimt often allowed
a single tree to occupy the
whole picture space. Here,
its contact with its
surroundings is reduced to
a low horizon along which
are seen the trunks of other
trees and the green grass
from which they spring.

Seeing Monet's work awakened Klimt to a different way
of seeing and also to the emotional qualities these new
techniques made possible. He recognized another means of
communicating ideas, which had been his intention with the
symbolic paintings, but which had been rejected by the
University commission.

In 1898 he painted his first landscapes, influenced by
Monet's broken brushwork and by his interest in water and
reflections and by the Japanese style of composition that had
been adopted by the Impressionists. However, Klimt did not
try for the same juxtapositions of primary colours of the Paris
painters. He was more interested in the mood induced by the
new technique of painting, a different way of communicating
of which James McNeill Whistler was a master.

In 1898 Klimt painted a picture called *Quiet Pond at
Schloss Kammer* (see also p.124), while staying with his friends
the Flöge family on the Attersee. The painting was of a tree
reflected in the water, with its shadow occupying most of the

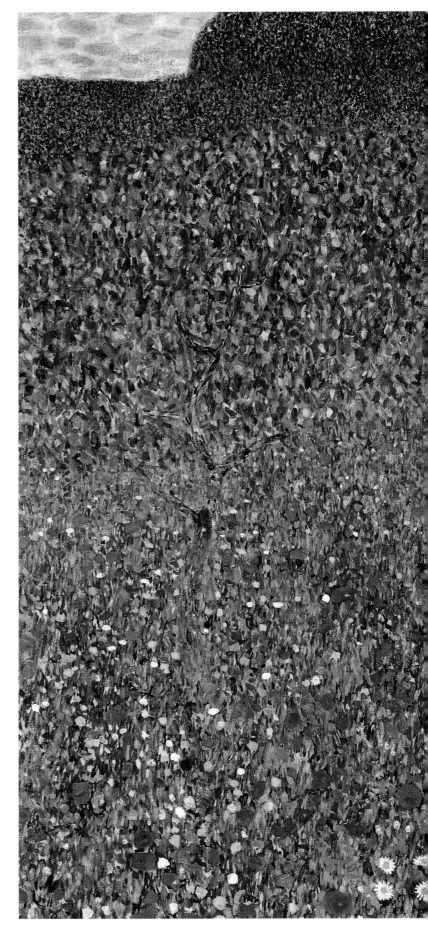

canvas area. It made no statement concerning nature or life, but it invited meditation.

The year 1900 saw *Farmhouse with Birch Trees* (p. 116–117), a painting without water, but with a large area of green grass with a few thin birch trees scattered over it, and with a horizon line so high in the canvas that the farmhouse is barely visible. He used the same disappearing horizon in *An Island on the Attersee* in which the island itself plays a small part in the composition which is dominated by the water of the lake.

Klimt was not aiming at the *plein-air* approach of an Impressionist painting but rather at a mood which evokes a feeling and invites contemplation. He had found a more effective way than symbolism for the aims which he was now pursuing, and he was concentrating more and more on creating an emotion or mood. He soon came to the conclusion that this could best be achieved by omitting extraneous and distracting objects; like Monet with his pond, Klimt's world shrank to close-up views which filled his whole

Poppy Field (1907)
Oil on canvas. 43 x 43in
(110$\frac{1}{3}$ x 110$\frac{1}{3}$cm).
Österreichische Galerie,
Vienna.

Klimt's poppy field has a
high horizon line which
keeps the viewer's eyes
firmly fixed on the earthy
foreground, though
suggesting a limitless
space beyond the trees.
For Klimt, nature had
become a potent means
of expressing his feelings
about life and the spirit.

Schloss Kammer on the Attersee III (1910)
Oil and canvas. 43¹/₃ x 43¹/₃in (110 x 110cm). Österreichische Galerie, Vienna.

Klimt painted this version of the Schloss Kammer for his friend and ertswhile lover, Adele Bloch-Bauer, whose portrait he had painted on

two occasions (p. 94–95 and 102). In this version of the château he has shown the picturesque façade screened by trees.

canvas. This microcosmic vision contained the larger world, a tree filling the whole of the square canvases that he preferred to use because he found the shape more conducive to restful contemplation.

A key painting was *The Golden Apple Tree*, which was destroyed in a fire at Schloss Immendorf in 1945. Gold symbolizes infinity and another dimension of existence, as it had to the medieval painters, who used it as a backdrop for their images of angels and saints. In Klimt's painting, the gold of the apples, glinting through the dark foliage of the tree, arouses similar feelings experienced when looking at the stars at night – those of hope and wonder.

In this way, Klimt began to develop a symbolic form of landscape. His woods and forests become infinite and impenetrable spaces full of mystery, the foliage of the trees enveloping the viewer to induce a feeling of oneness with nature. His wild flowers are scattered all over the canvas

Orchard with Roses

(1911–12)

Oil and canvas. 43⅓ x
43⅓in (110 x 110)cm.
Private collection.

This busy garden,
showing nature in all its
abundance, has not been
left to its own devices to
grow and spread at will,
but shows evidence of a
human hand which cares
for the orchard and roses
without subduing their
innate vitality.

with the same vitality of natural growth as in his paintings
Farm Garden with Sunflowers (p. 68) or *Roses under the Trees*
(p. 118 and 119). Klimt's sunflowers differ from Van Gogh's
(which emphasize the sun's dominance over all life), having
their own personal mood, and are executed in a method the
Expressionists would use to project their emotions.

In 1909 Klimt visited Paris and discovered the Cubist
experiments of Picasso and Braque. The process was too
intellectual and analytical for Klimt but he was interested in

Farm Garden with Crucifix (1911–12)
Oil on canvas. 43 x 43in (110$\frac{1}{3}$ x 110$\frac{1}{3}$cm).

This painting was once in the collection of August Lederer but was destroyed by a fire at the Immendorf Palace in 1945. It has much in common with Van Gogh's feelings of intimacy with nature and reveals Klimt's own concern to express himself through landscape.

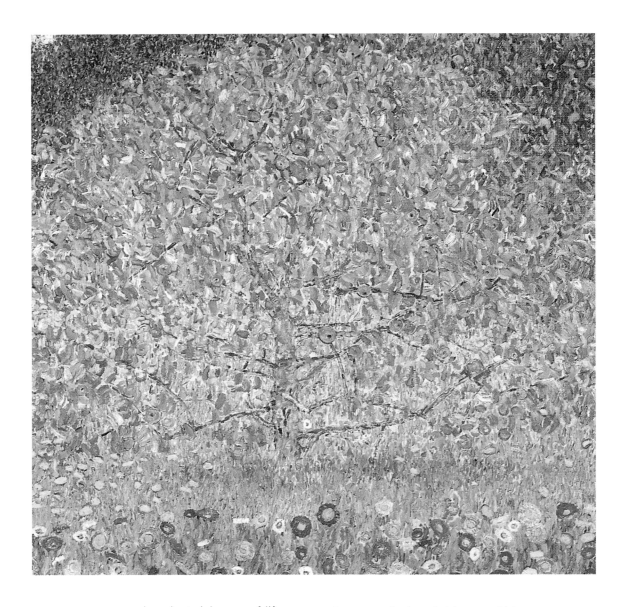

Apple Tree I (c.1912)
Oil on canvas. 43^1/$_3$ x
43^1/$_3$in (110 x 110cm).
Österreichsche Galerie,
Vienna.

Apple trees held a
particular meaning for
Klimt who saw in their
golden fruit all the
abundant richness of life.
The fruit, shining like suns
or stars in the depths of
the dark foliage, are the
universal symbols of light
shining through the
darkness, or truth through
obscurity, and assume an
almost sacred dimension.

the strength that Cubism could impart to a composition. On
his return to Austria, he began to paint landscapes that
included houses and villages on the Attersee (see p. 132).
Schloss Kammer has a distinct echo of villages and houses
painted by the Cubists in Provence; but Klimt's landscapes
are green with trees, the houses are part of nature and two-
dimensional, because Klimt was interested in the patterns of
life more than in the structure of matter.

Klimt painted over 50 landscapes between 1897 and his
death in 1918. They represent one fifth of his total output
and form the most significant part of his work in the 20th
century. Today, his reputation rests largely on these works,
perhaps because they are the most accessible part of his
oeuvre; though not everyone with an attractive Klimt print
in their house or on their office wall will realize that behind
the pretty picture lies a whole philosophy of life.

Garden Path with Chickens (1916)
Oil on canvas. 43$^{1}/_{3}$ x 43$^{1}/_{3}$in (110 x 110cm). Destroyed by a fire at the Immendorf Palace in 1945.

The path through the hollyhocks is reminiscent of Monet's painting of a path bordered by sunflowers in a garden at Vétheuil, though Klimt's flowers are more clearly delineated with dark paint. The darker, heavier tones, when compared with the picture on a similar theme on page 115, may be due to Klimt's more sombre mood, possibly attributable to war.

129

Apple Tree II (1916)
Oil on canvas. 43$\frac{1}{3}$ x 43$\frac{1}{3}$in (110 x 110cm). Österreichisches Galerie, Vienna.

In this painting, the entire tree practically fills the canvas, its yellow apples shimmering among their dark foliage like stars. Klimt has lightly treated the row of background trees so as not to distract from the main subject and its overwhelming fruitfulness. Unlike Cézanne, who looked for structure in nature, Klimt was more concerned with the patterns and textures to be discerned in the plants and landscapes around him.

Houses in Unterach on Lake Atter (c.1916)
Oil on canvas. 43$\frac{1}{3}$ x 43$\frac{1}{3}$in (110 x 100cm). Österreichisches Galerie, Vienna.

Klimt spent most of the First World War years on the Attersee, at the home of Emilie Flöge and her family. But even in this peaceful place he was aware of the death and destruction elsewhere.

Not only that, there were intimations that the days of the once-glorious Austro-Hungarian Empire were numbered. He was now well into his 50s and had decided to seek solace in nature in a

tranquil setting, where he could enjoy the company of friends, choose his subjects, and paint at will.

Avenue in the Park of Schloss Kammer (1912)
Oil on canvas. 43$^{1}/_{3}$ x 43$^{1}/_{3}$in (110 x 110cm). Österreichisches Galerie, Vienna.

This is another view of Schloss Kammer (see also p. 124) which Klimt painted several times, mostly from the lake. He clearly enjoyed this as an exercise in both the symmetric and the asymmetric, the château appearing off-centre framed by the swirling, overlapping trees with their dark, somewhat forbidding forms.

CHAPTER EIGHT
AFTER KLIMT

Self-Portrait: Oskar Kokoschka (1917)
Oil on canvas. 26¹/₂ x
17¹/₂in (67.5 x 44.5cm)
Heydt Museum,
Wuppertal.

Kokoschka produced this
self-portrait after he had
been released from the
army following a severe
head wound. His pre-war
leanings towards an

In the years preceding the Great War, Klimt was an
acknowledged master and much revered in Austria, though
he was little known in the rest of Europe because his
evolution as a painter had occurred away from the influential
school of Paris, where the post-Impressionists ruled as the
new avant-garde. The French were in the throes of an
intellectual exploration of the potential of structure and
colour, with the opposing forces soon to be recognized as the
Fauves or Cubists.

In Austria, Germany and Scandinavia, other forces were at
work, grouped together under the banner of Expressionism.
The liberation of inner impulses and the traumas of the soul,
encouraged by Freudian introspection, was the tide that
moved young artists in these northern European countries.
Klimt had been a fringe member of the Expressionist
movement with his symbolic paintings, but his objectivity and
reserve, as much as his age, prevented him from giving way to

Expressionist style now
became more marked, his
brushstrokes broader and
more violent, and traces
of the Klimt influence
were beginning to
disappear. He began to
travel and absorb the art
of painters in other parts
of Europe and in the
process developed a
distinctive style of his
own.

134

Mother with Two Children (Egon Schiele, 1917)
Oil on canvas. 59 x 62$\frac{1}{2}$in (150 x 158.7cm). Österreichische Galerie, Vienna.

Schiele's neurotic vision is not as evident in this painting of a mother with her children as it is in his nudes. The manner in which the figures are merged into one form is derived from Klimt, though the handling of the patches of colour lacks the freedom of the master's work. The tension displayed on the mother's face is typical of Schiele's subjective Expressionism.

Death and the Maiden
(Egon Schiele,1915)
Oil on canvas. 59 x 71in
(150 x 180cm).
Österreichische Galerie,
Vienna.

Egon Schiele was Klimt's
pupil and has borrowed a
theme from a picture,
Death and Life (p. 76),
which Klimt had started in
about 1911 and which he
was in the process of
repainting. In the original
version, Klimt used a gold
leaf background, but had
replaced it with a painted
one. It was a morbid
subject that appealed to
both men who were
haunted by the darker
sides of life, even in their
more cheerful paintings.
Schiele's version is less
symbolic and more
realistic than Klimt's and
suggests a sombre and
neurotic actuality.

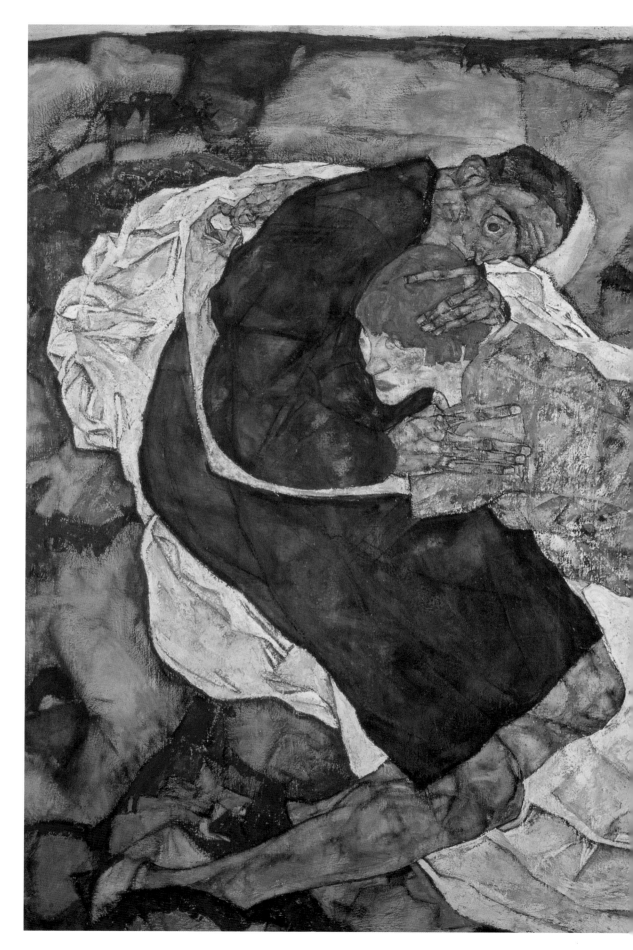

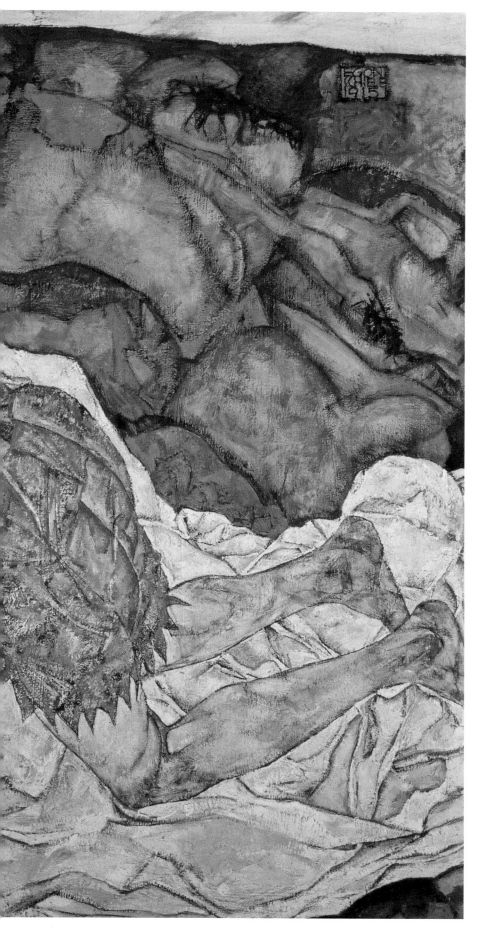

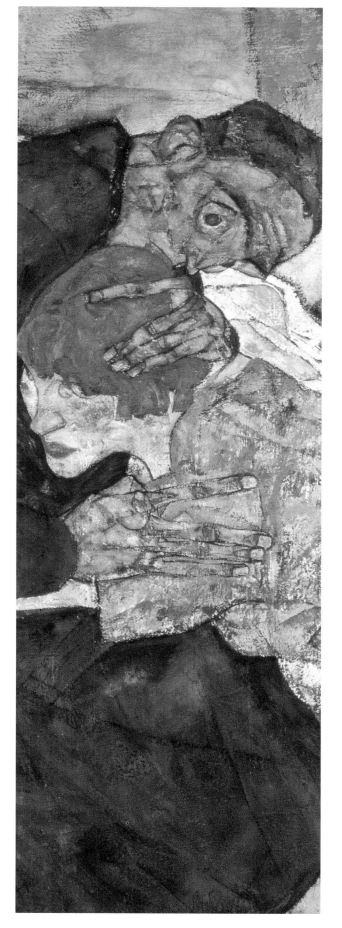

Poster for the Vienna Secession's 49th Exhibition: Die Freunde
(Egon Schiele, 1918)
Colour lithograph. 25 x 19in (63.5 x 48cm).
The Fitzwilliam Museum, University of Cambridge, England.

The style of Schiele's poster is very different from his nudes and harks back to the comradeship of the Secession artists before the war, which was the end of Austria as they knew it. However, it also celebrated their success in changing the course of art in their own country.

the surge of liberating subjectivity felt by the young on the eve of the Great War. This was not the case with two talented painters, Oskar Kokoschka and Egon Schiele, who were to all intents and purposes Klimt's students, and who expected to take his place as the leaders of the new art which had begun with the Secessionist revolt of the 1890s.

The elder of the two by four years was Oskar Kokoschka (born in 1886), the son of a goldsmith from lower Austria who plied his business in Vienna. Kokoschka, like Klimt, had been a student at the Kunstgewerbeschule and had exhibited his work at the Kunstchau, the annual art show which had become more important than the Salon. Kokoschka's vigorous handling of paint failed to gain the approval of Vienna's art critics, who considered his work crass. Klimt supported the young artist, who had been his pupil between 1904 and 1909, claiming that talent was more important than tastefulness: having established a friendship and understanding with Kokoschka, he invited him to exhibit again at the following Kunstchau, which Klimt himself was organizing. Kokoschka, who also wrote poetry and drama, expressed his gratitude in a poem inscribed 'To Gustav Klimt, in admiration'.

Times were changing in Vienna and the affluent middle classes who had been Klimt's patrons were becoming increasingly perturbed by the influx of the poor arriving in Austria's capital in search of work. The elegant and ordered existence of Viennese life was being threatened by an invasion of strangers who added to the numbers of unemployed and had no appreciation for the established life of the city which was in a slow and inexorable state of flux. Though Klimt was aware of the changes, they did not affect him as much as they did the younger artists, for he had for some years retired from the life of the capital and sequestered himself among the lakes of the Salzkammergut, where he painted large numbers of landscapes.

For younger men like Kokoschka and Schiele, the life of polite Viennese society was irrelevant. They were aware of the poverty and misery of large sections of the population and the futile attempts of the Emperor Franz Joseph's governments to shore up the past. Moreover, the troubles in the Balkan territories, which the Austro-Hungarian Empire had acquired in the 1870s, added to the general discontent of young people with the established world as it existed at the time.

Reclining Nude in Green Stockings (Egon Schiele, 1914)
Watercolour and pencil.
12 x 18in (30.5 x 46cm).
Private Collection.

This is typical of Schiele nudes, which often seem to inhabit a grey area between repulsion and pornography. The emphasis on the wide-eyed head and the pubic hair is erotic, but the unsympathetic line of the recumbent body has a repugnant quality, suggesting that the artist was feeling a mixture of lust and revulsion before the naked woman. If the intention was symbolic of the concept of life as a doomed journey for men and women, it was quite unlike Klimt's own optimistic feelings on the subject.

Self-Portrait: Oskar Kokoschka (1910)
Lithograph. 28 x 18½in (70.9 x 47cm).
Private collection.

Kokoschka worked with Klimt as a young man and was influenced by his notions of a new art, though his development was along Expressionist lines that were prevalent in Germany. The Expressionists emphasized the emotional aspects of a subject, whereas Klimt preferred to express himself by symbolic means, remaining objective rather than subjective. Of the two, however, Kokoschka's was the more volatile nature.

Kokoschka used the children of the new poor, often underfed and badly clothed, as his models and his sympathy for their condition introduced a note of hard realism which had hitherto not been seen in Austrian art. These same children of the poor also posed for Egon Schiele, whose admiration for Klimt was first ignited when he met him at the Kunstgewerbeschule that Klimt and Kokoschka had attended. There was thus a link between the three men that bridged the generation gap. Klimt appreciated the talent of the young students and they, though very different in their views of life, admired his skills.

Of the two younger artists, Schiele was the more obsessively attached to Klimt and was the more influenced by his technique and themes. Not unnaturally flattered by a brilliant student's adulation, Klimt encouraged him to exhibit at the Kunstchau. Schiele, however, had a very different temperament from Klimt. He was a tortured, neurotic young man, unsure of his identity and with deep anxieties concerning the world about him. His brilliant draughtsmanship reveals his inner turmoil, especially in the nudes which, following Klimt's example, he adopted as the main subjects of his drawings.

Both young men, destined to be true artists of the future, were products of the new society that was replacing Klimt's generation. Both were destined to experience the collapse of Austria in 1918 when dreams were to be forever shattered, and which put an end to the city of street concerts and the waltz. The experience of Kokoschka and Schiele was to be mirrored in the work of artists of other Secessionist movements in Munich, Dresden and Berlin.

The need to express ideas and feelings that had long been suppressed in a tightly regulated society had appeared in Klimt's symbolism. Now it was coming into the open, fed by the fires of individualistic and often neurotic artists such as Edvard Munch and James Ensor, who were obsessed with death and decay in a more forceful and immediate way than had been the case before. In the course of its appearances on the art scene, Expressionism passed briefly through the art of Klimt during his symbolic period when death and morbid sex were frequent visitors to his paintings.

This new manner of painting spread throughout Europe, infecting artists with an inner sense of doom concerning the future. It was a kind of painting that allowed emotions to be displayed in the raw state and had a long lineage, stretching back to Mathis Grünewald's Crucified Christ. In our own era, it has found its strongest expression in the work of artists such as Francis Bacon and Lucien Freud.

Two Nudes (The Lovers)
(Oskar Kokoschka, 1913)
Oil on canvas. 64$\frac{1}{4}$ x
38$\frac{1}{3}$in (163 x 97.5cm).
Museum of Fine Arts,
Boston, Mass.

The Lovers was painted
soon after the artist met
Alma Mahler, wife of the
composer, Gustav Mahler.
Kokoschka was artistically
close to Klimt and no
doubt influenced by his
device of using embracing
couples to suggest the
idea of universal love.
Moreover, Kokoschka
nudes show a disturbing
earthiness when
compared with Klimt's
idealized couples. The
emphatic planes which
describe the forms of the
figures show a leaning
towards Cézanne or
Cubist influences.